Mel Bay Presents

Bluegrass & Country Guitar for the Young Beginner

By William Bay

CD CONTENTS

2 3 4 5 6 7 8 9 0

Holding the Guitar

Position the guitar so that you are comfortable. The right hand should rest over the sound hole. The left hand should be able to reach the first fret.

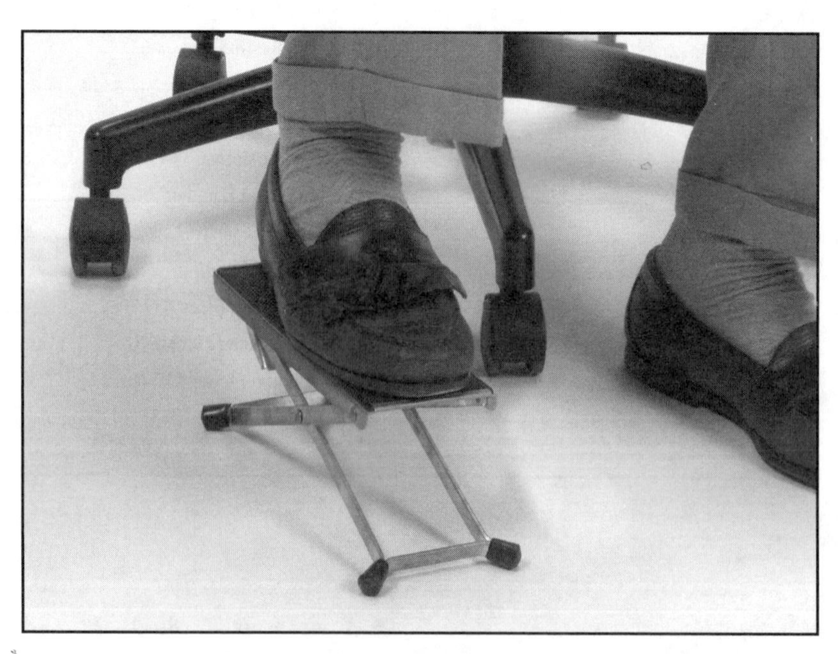

A footstool can be purchased at your local music store. The footstool is adjustable and can help elevate the guitar to a comfortable height.

Placing the Left Hand on the Guitar

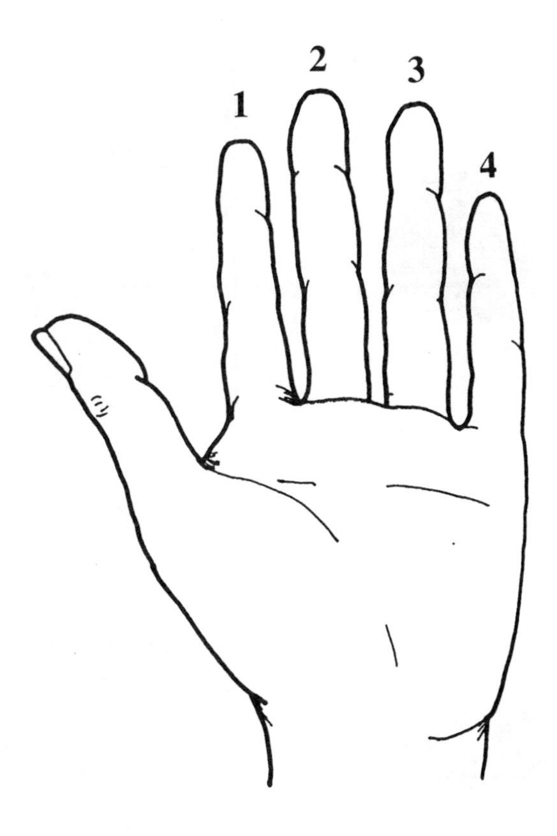

Left Hand Position

Place your fingers firmly on the strings directly behind the frets. The thumb should be placed in the center of the back of the neck. Do not wrap your thumb around the neck.

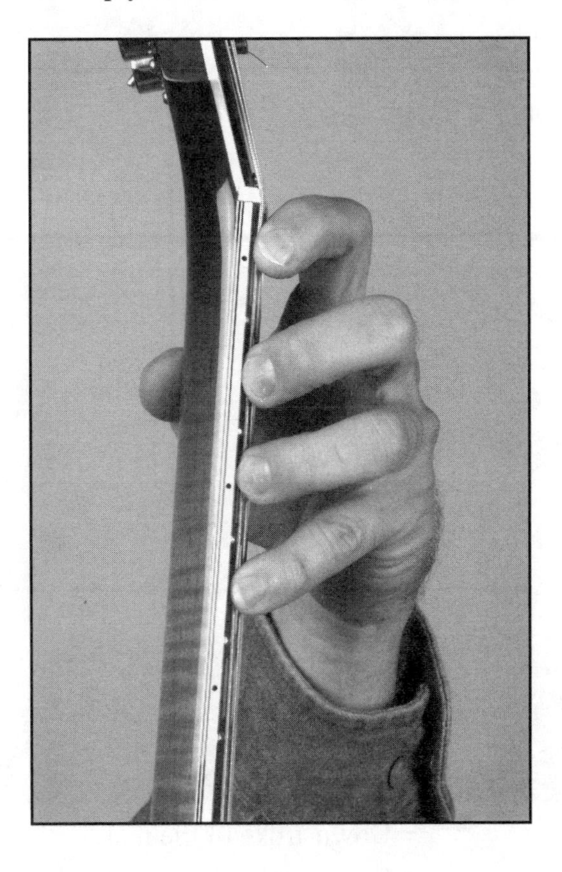

Holding the Pick

Flatpicks

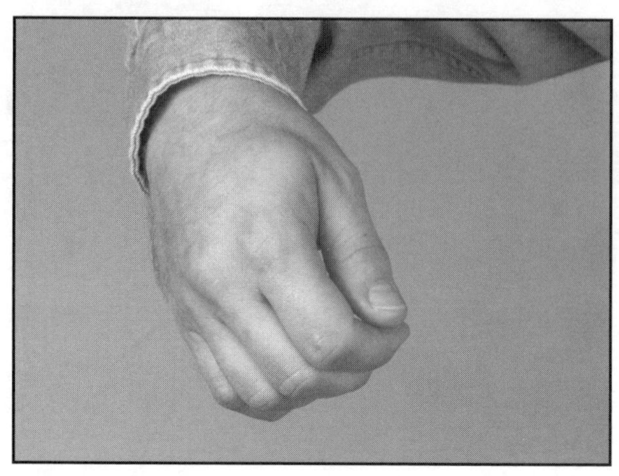

The right hand fingers are curved.
Keep the hand loose–not rigid.

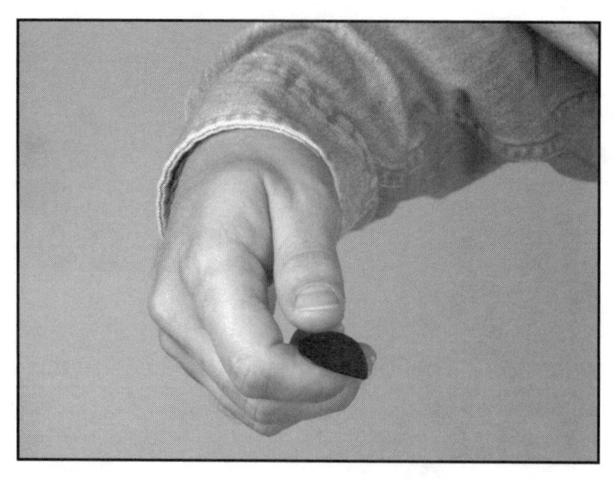

The pick rests gently on the index finger with the "point" aiming away from the thumb.

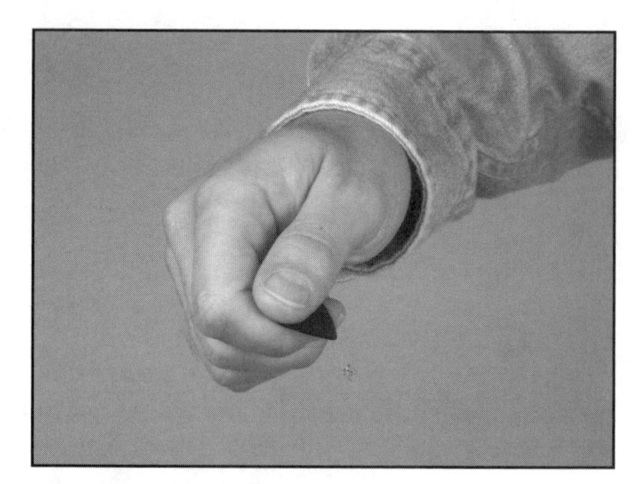

The thumb rests on top of the pick to hold it in place.

⊓ = Downstroke of the pick.

Parts of the Guitar

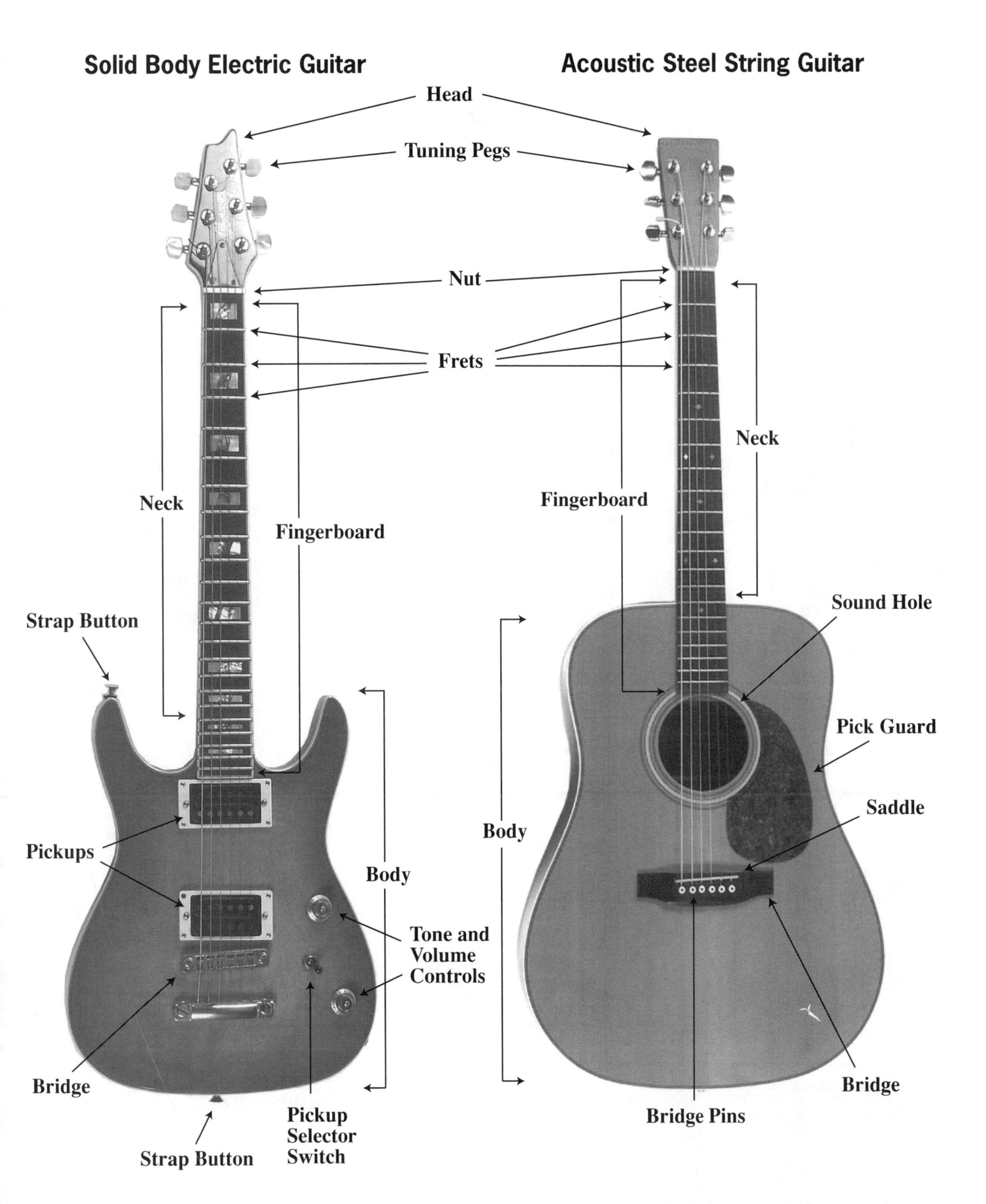

Solid Body Electric Guitar
Acoustic Steel String Guitar
Head
Tuning Pegs
Nut
Frets
Neck
Fingerboard
Neck
Fingerboard
Strap Button
Sound Hole
Pick Guard
Saddle
Body
Pickups
Body
Tone and Volume Controls
Bridge
Bridge
Bridge Pins
Pickup Selector Switch
Strap Button

Tuning the Guitar

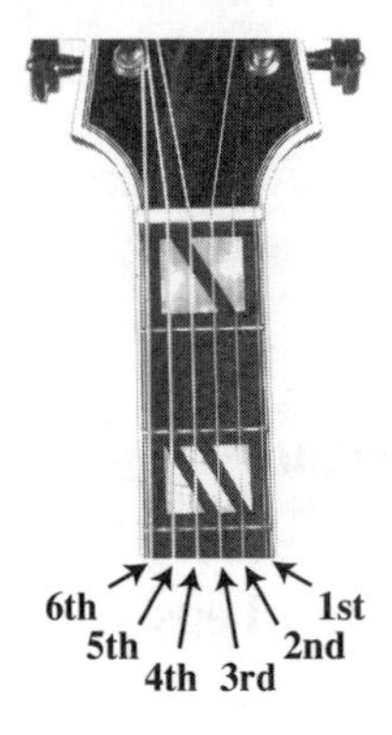

1 **Listen to track #1 of your CD and tune up as follows!**

1st String – E

2nd String – B

3rd String – G

4th String – D

5th String – A

6th String – Low E

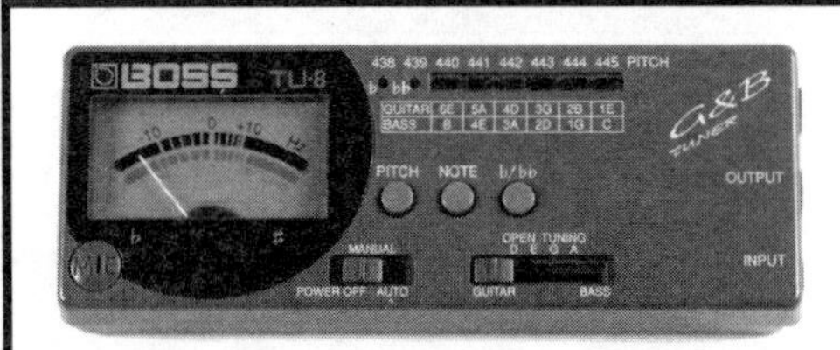

Electronic Guitar Tuner

Electronic Guitar Tuners are available at your music store. They are a handy device and highly recommended.

Strumming

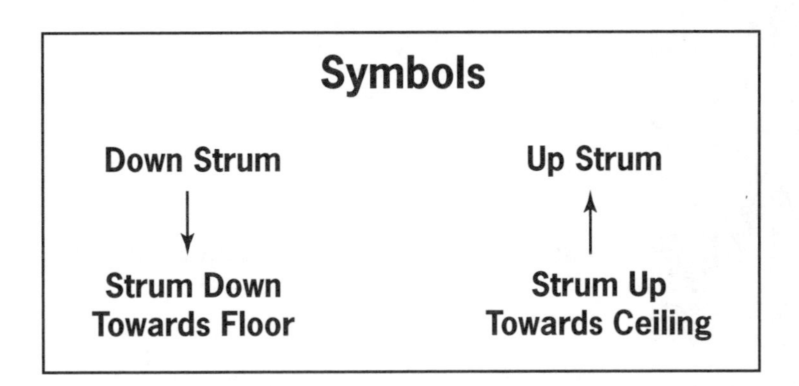

Symbols
Down Strum
Strum Down
Towards Floor
Up Strum
Strum Up
Towards Ceiling

Using a Pick

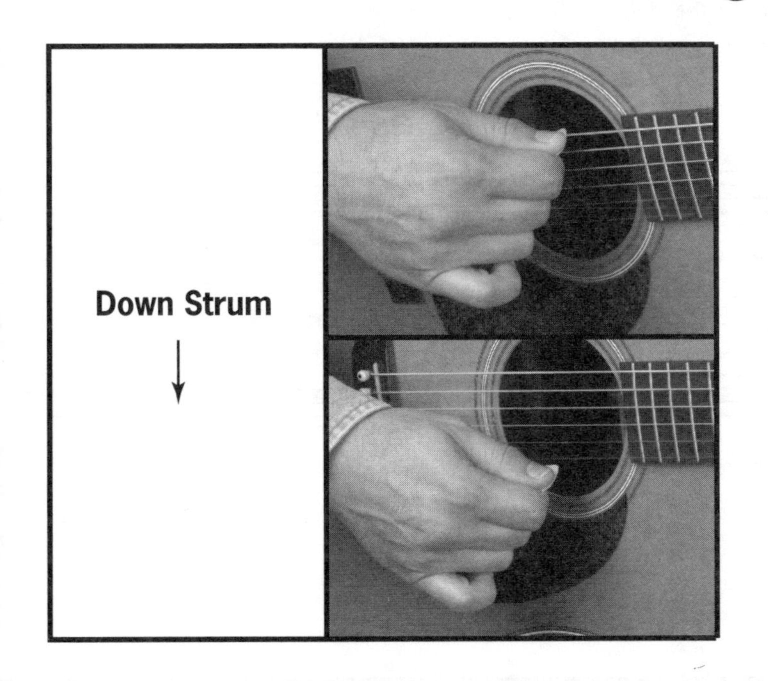

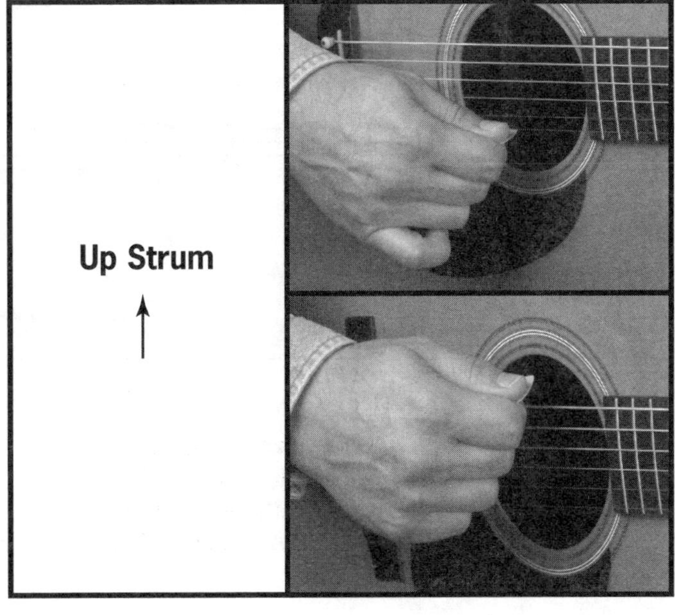

Our First Two Chords

G/EZ Form

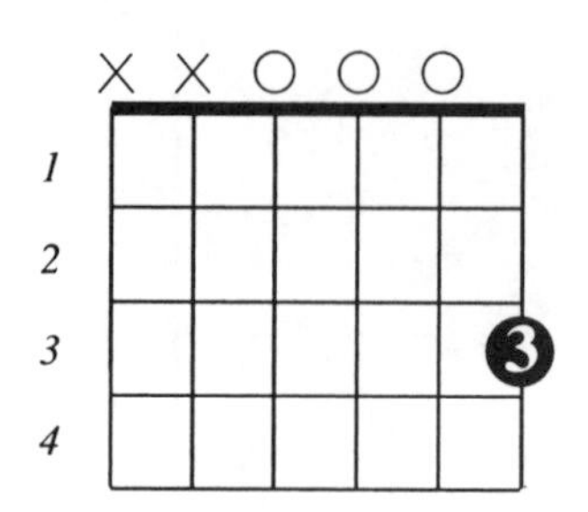
1
2
3
4

The Farmer in the Dell

CD Track Number

2

Starting Pitch

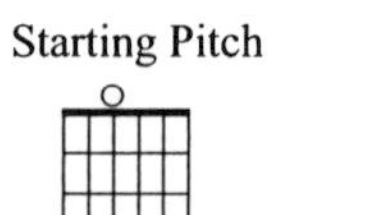

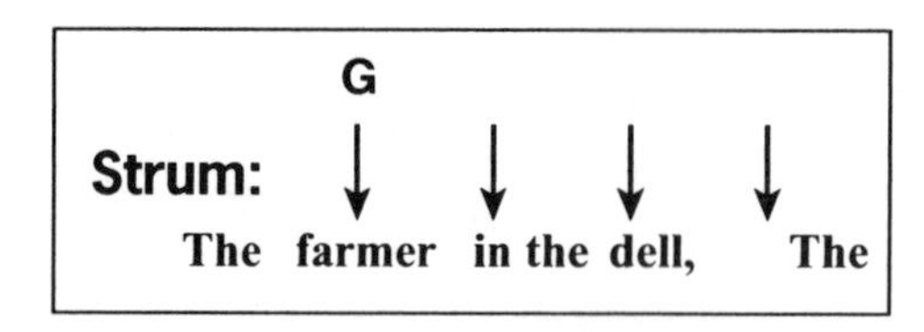
G
Strum:
The farmer in the dell, The

Folk Song

G
The far - mer in the dell, The far - mer in the dell,
Heigh, ho, the der - ry o! The far - mer in the dell!

2. The farmer takes a wife
3. The wife takes a child
4. The child takes a nurse
5. The nurse takes a dog
6. The dog takes a cat.
7. The cat takes a rat.
8. The rat takes the cheese.
9. The cheese stands alone.

D7 Chord

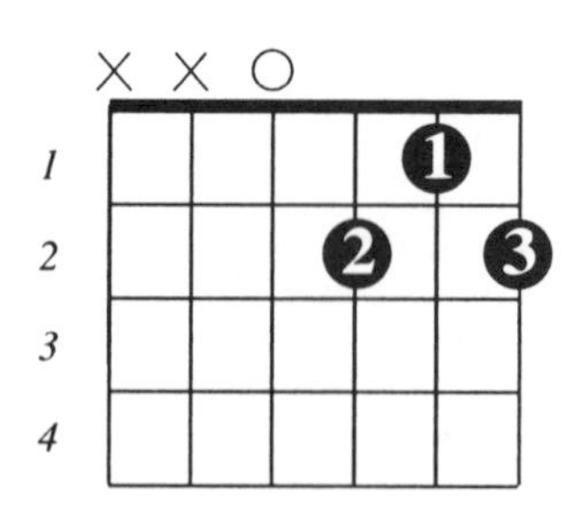
1
2
3
4

Strum Practice

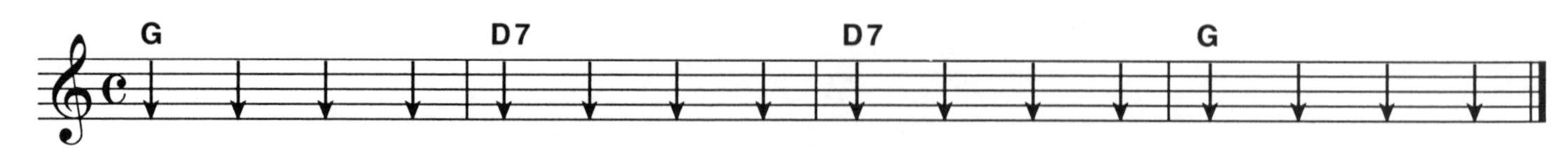
G
D7
D7
G

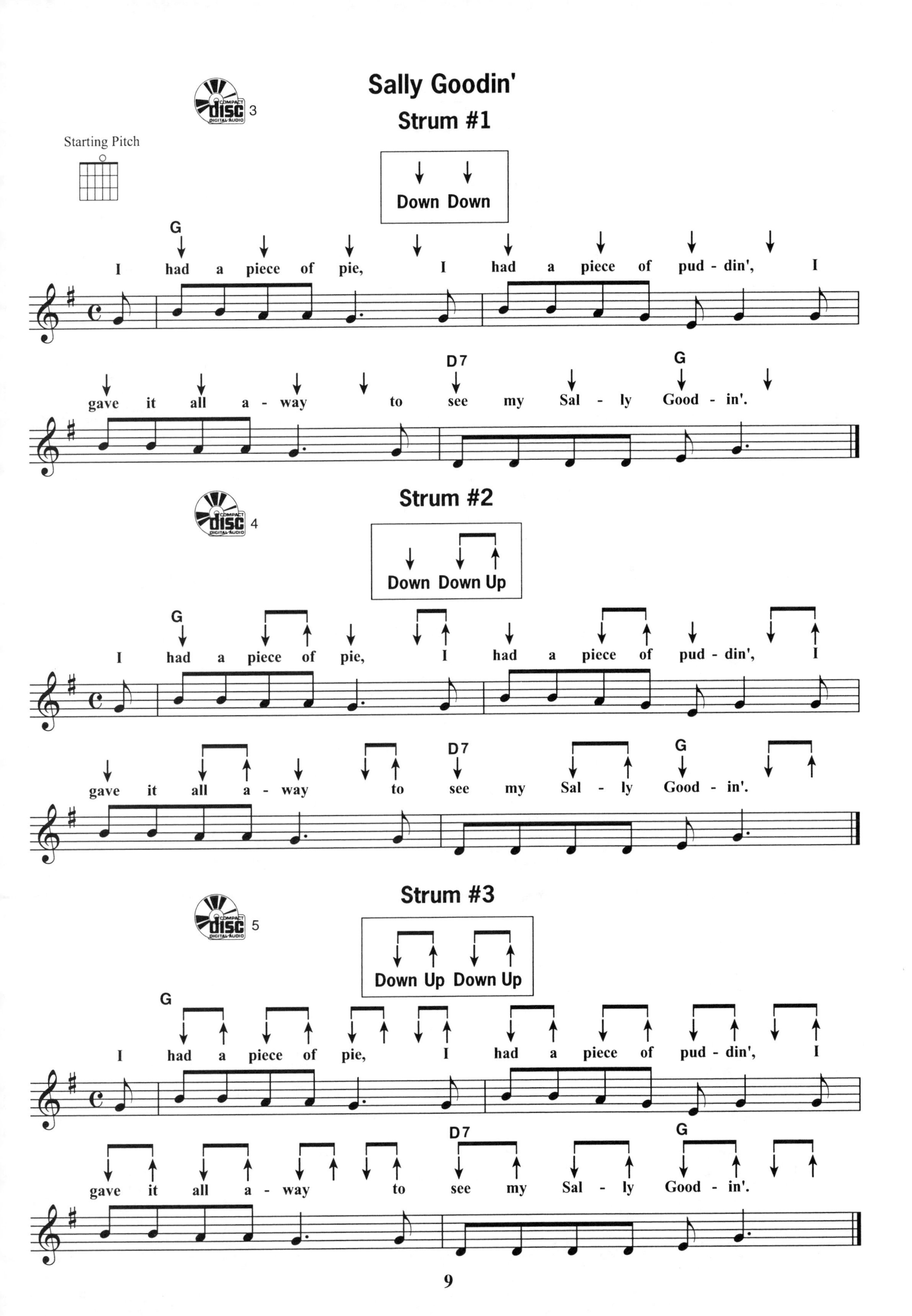
Sally Goodin'
Strum #1
3
Starting Pitch
Down Down
G
I had a piece of pie, I had a piece of pud - din', I
D7
G
gave it all a - way to see my Sal - ly Good - in'.
Strum #2
4
Down Down Up
G
I had a piece of pie, I had a piece of pud - din', I
D7
G
gave it all a - way to see my Sal - ly Good - in'.
Strum #3
5
Down Up Down Up
G
I had a piece of pie, I had a piece of pud - din', I
D7
G
gave it all a - way to see my Sal - ly Good - in'.
9

Old Chisholm Trail

Bury Me Not on the Lone Prairie

Full G Chord

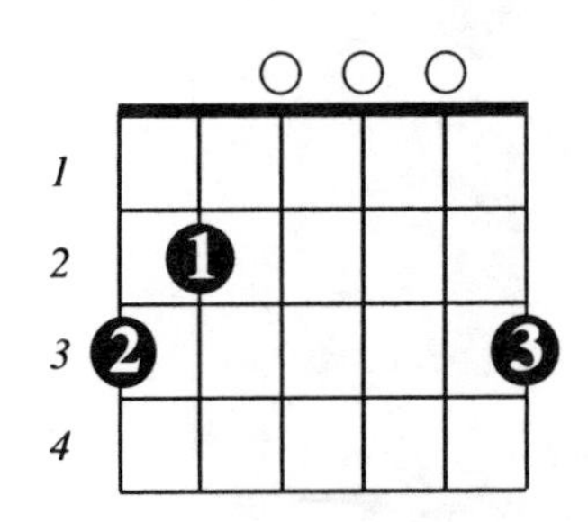
1
2
3
4
1
2
3

Leather Britches

Starting Pitch

8

G
Lit - tle boy, lit - tle boy where'd you get your britch - es.
D7
G
Dad - dy cut 'em out and mom - my sewed the stitch - es.

My Home's Across the Smoky Mountains

9

Starting Pitch

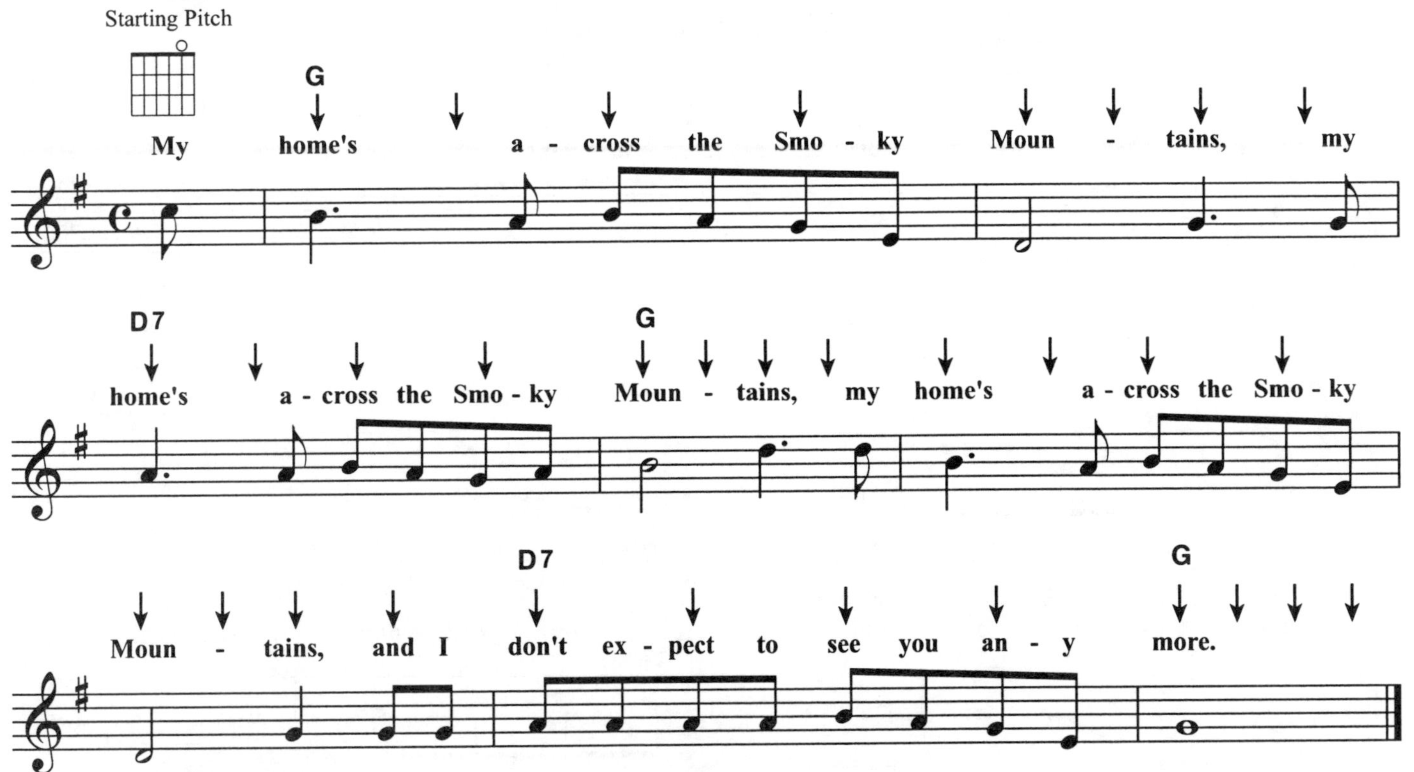
G
My home's a - cross the Smo - ky Moun - tains, my
D7
G
home's a - cross the Smo - ky Moun - tains, my home's a - cross the Smo - ky
D7
G
Moun - tains, and I don't ex - pect to see you an - y more.

C Chord

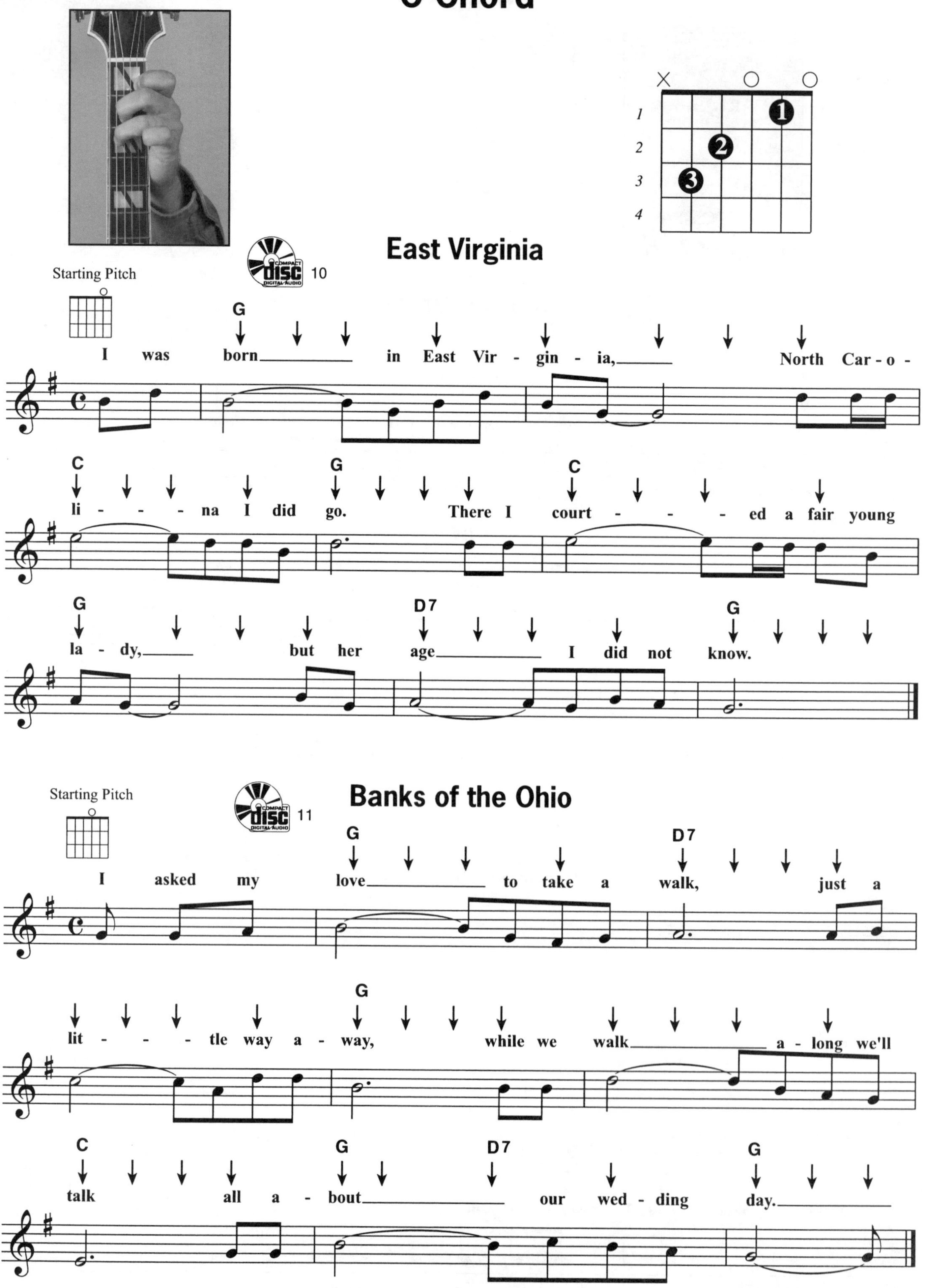
1
2
3
4
East Virginia
Starting Pitch
10
G
I was born in East Vir - gin - ia, North Car - o -
C G C
li - - - na I did go. There I court - - - ed a fair young
G D7 G
la - dy, but her age I did not know.
Banks of the Ohio
Starting Pitch
11
G D7
I asked my love to take a walk, just a
G
lit - - - tle way a - way, while we walk a - long we'll
C G D7 G
talk all a - bout our wed - ding day.

3/4 Time

In 3/4 Time We Count 3 Beats per Measure

Strum Practice

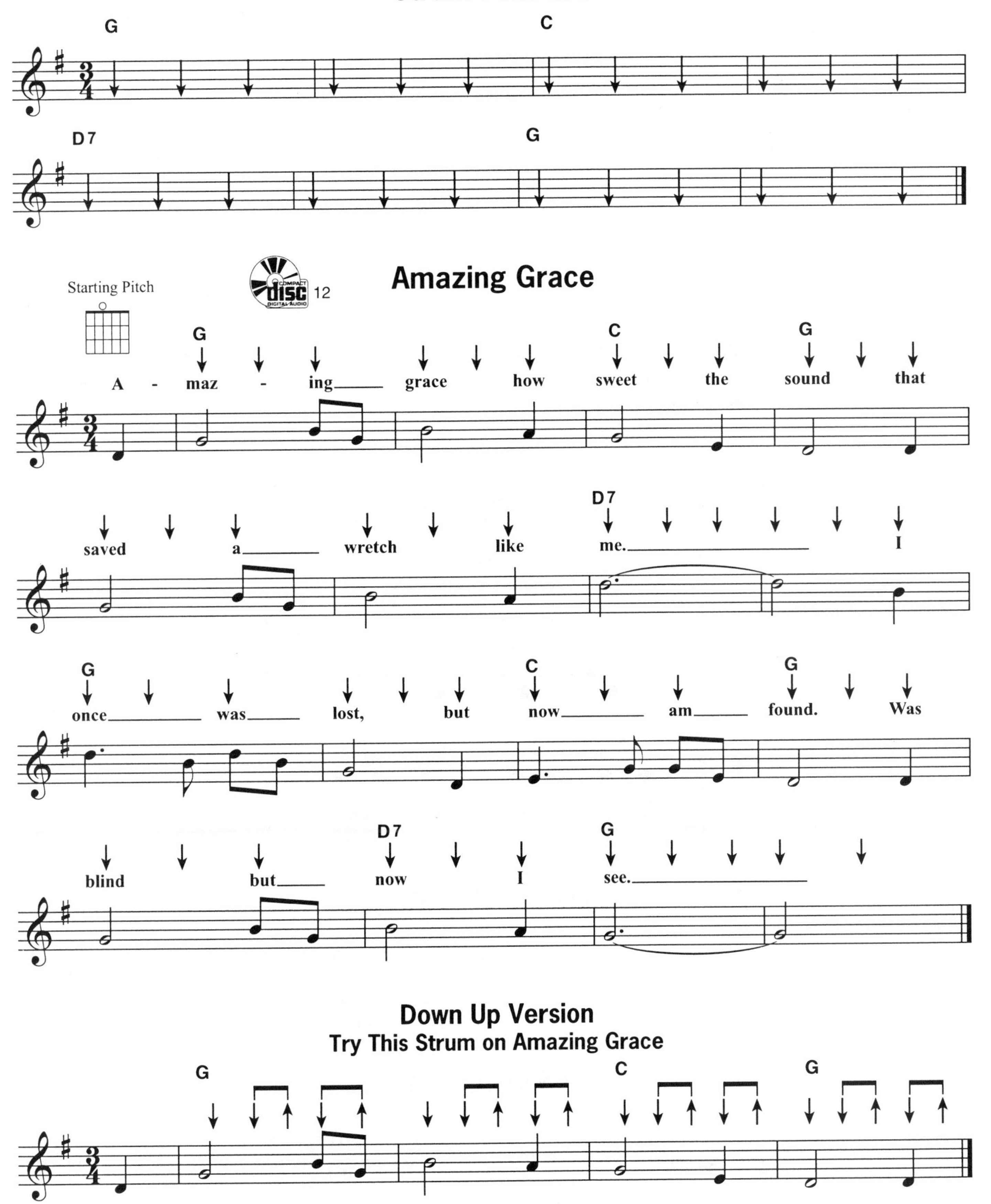

Types of Notes

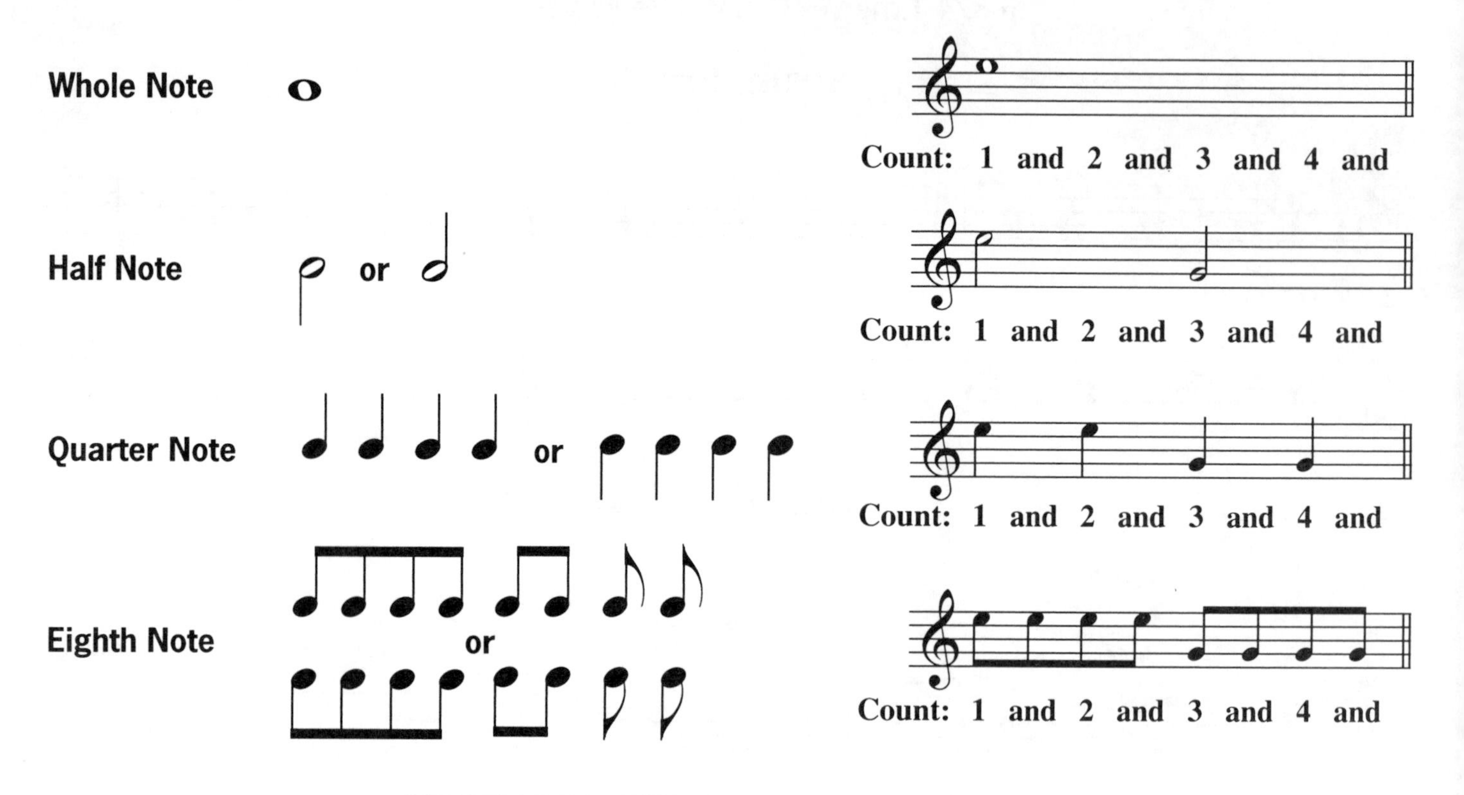

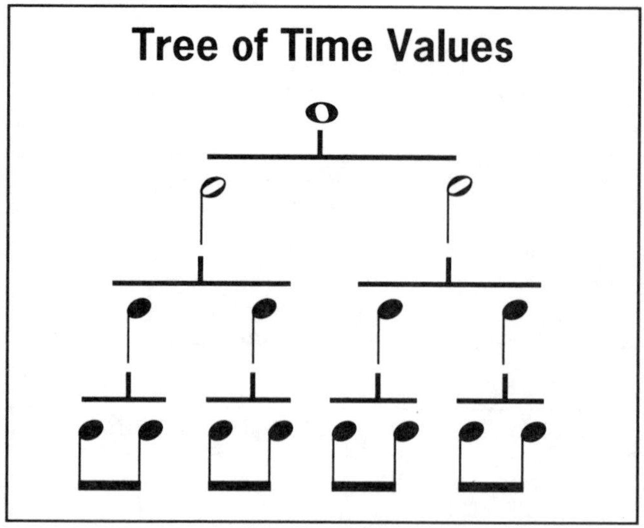

Dotted Half Note

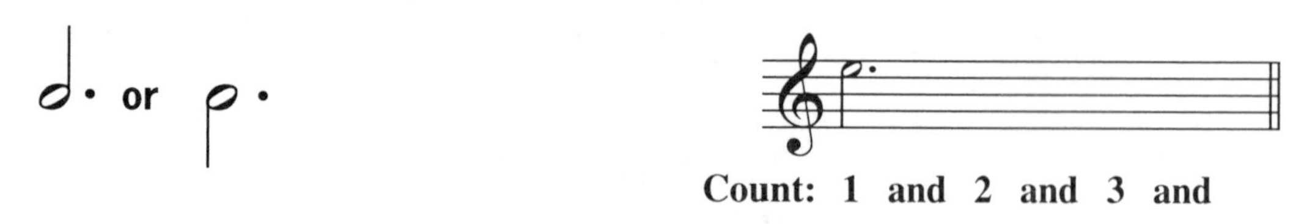

Dotted Quarter Note

Note Review

Play the following studies on the open E string (first string).

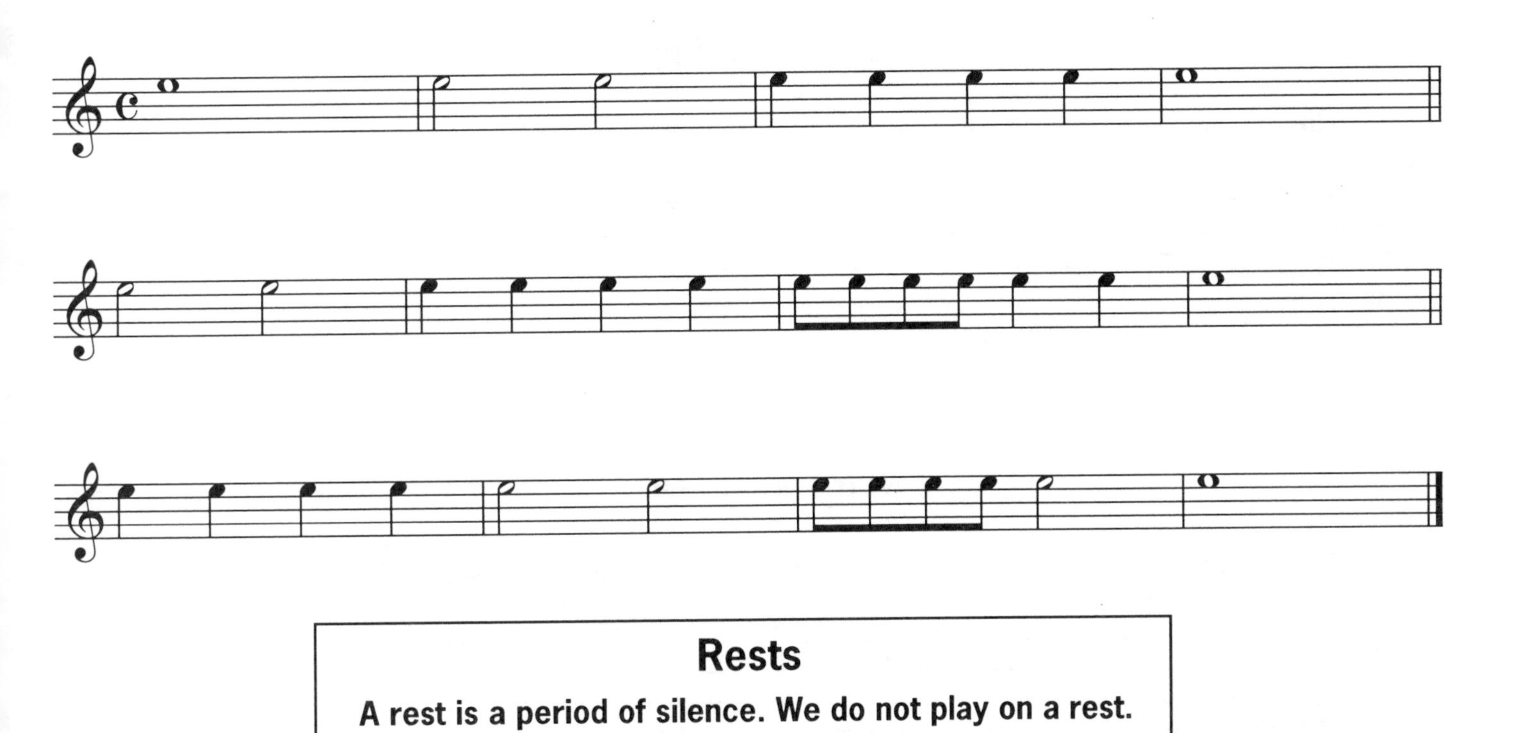

Tabs

Tablature is a way of writing guitar music which shows you *where* to play the notes.

Lines = Strings

1st String
2nd String
3rd String
4th String
5th String
6th String

Numbers = Frets

1st String Open — 0
2nd String, 1st Fret — 1
3rd String, 2nd Fret — 2
5th String Open — 0

S T R I N G ① ② ③ ④ ⑤ ⑥

Tab Time Values

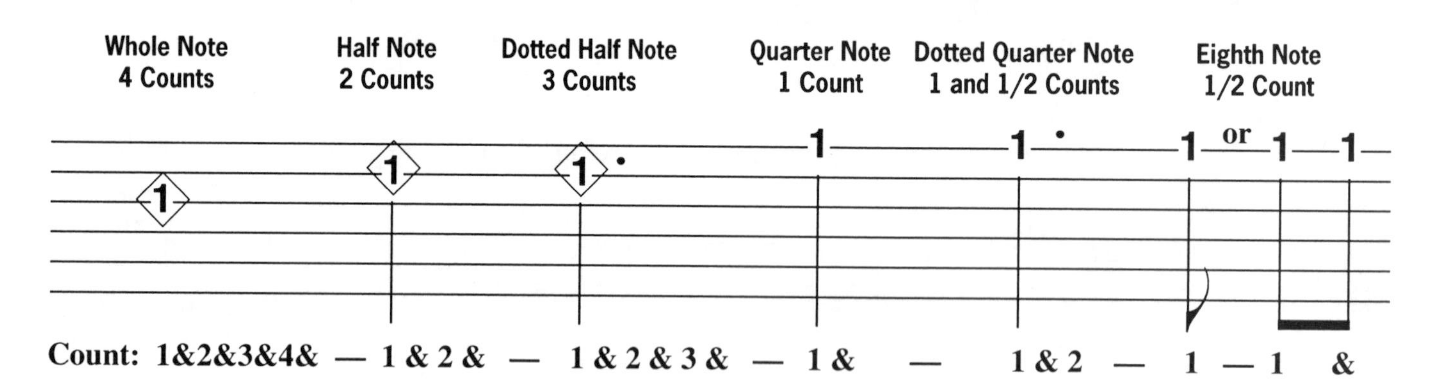

Tab Review

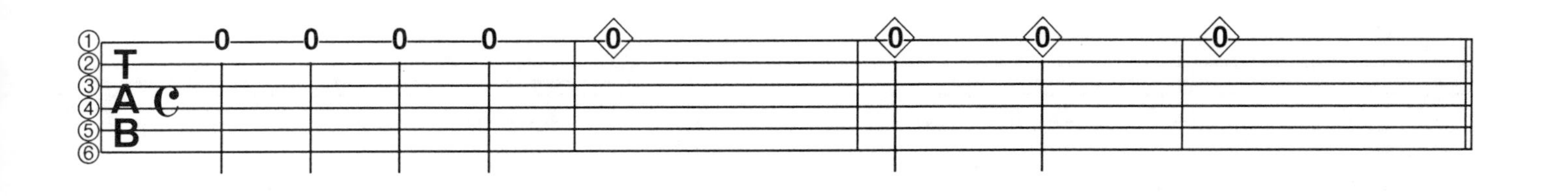

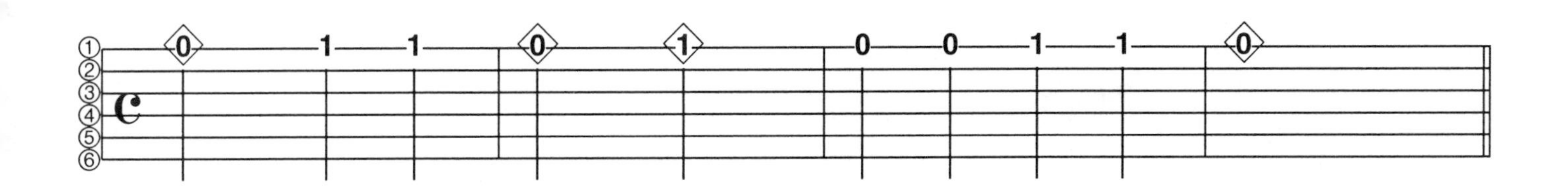

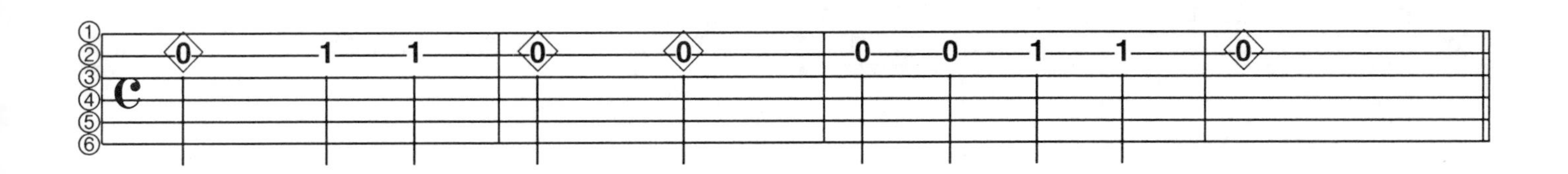

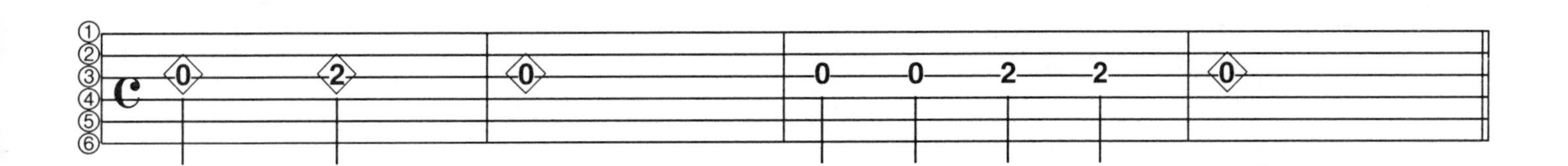

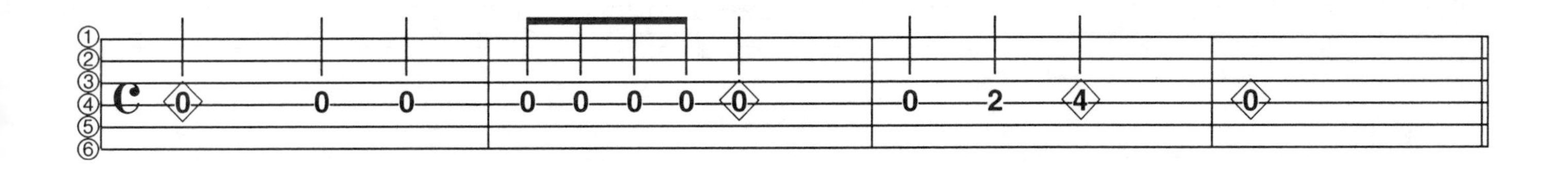

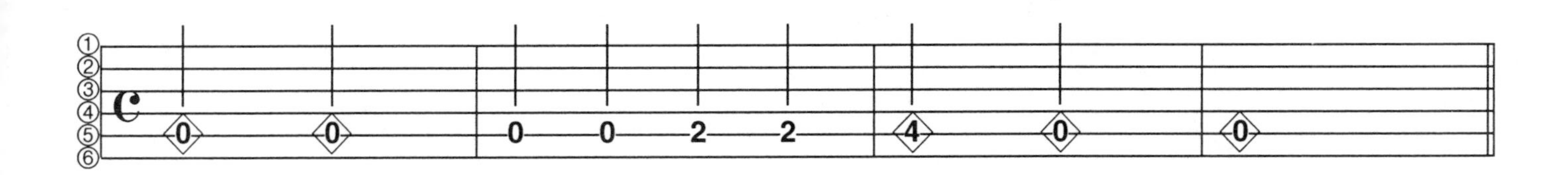

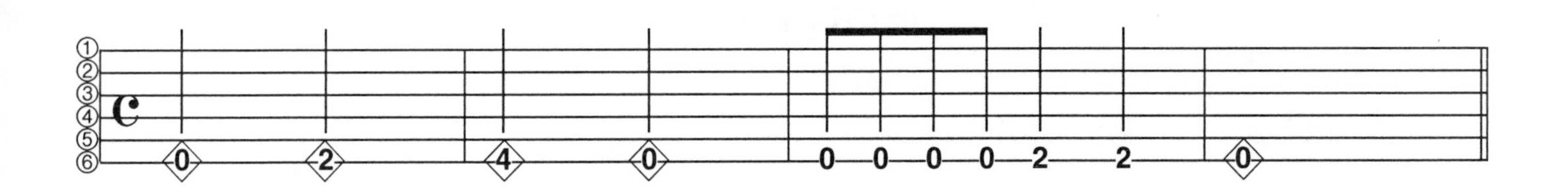

Jack of Diamonds
Notes to learn

2. I'll eat when I'm hungry
I'll drink when I'm dry,
And when I get thirsty
I'll lay down and cry.

My Home's Across the Smoky Montains

(New Accompaniment)

New Note

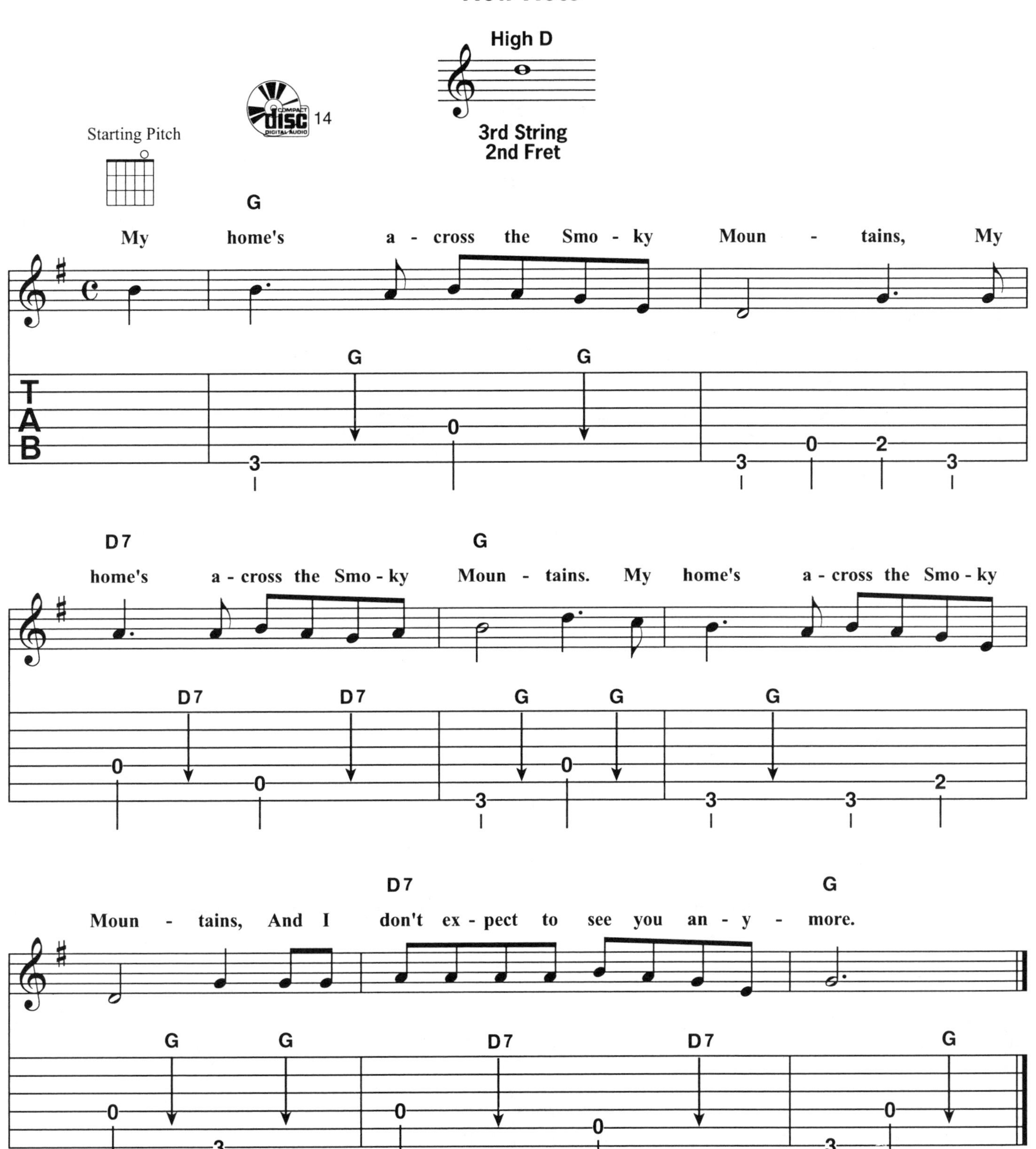

High D
3rd String
2nd Fret
14
Starting Pitch
G
My home's a - cross the Smo - ky Moun - tains, My
G G
0
3 3 0 2 3
D7 G
home's a - cross the Smo - ky Moun - tains. My home's a - cross the Smo - ky
D7 D7 G G G
0 0 3 0 3 3 2
D7 G
Moun - tains, And I don't ex - pect to see you an - y - more.
G G D7 D7 G
0 3 0 0 3 0

2. How can I keep from crying
How can I keep from crying
How can I keep from crying
For I never expect to see you anymore

3. Rock and feed my baby candy
Rock and feed my baby candy
Rock and feed my baby candy
For I never expect to see you anymore

4. Goodbye my little darling
Goodbye my little darling
Goodbye my little darling
For I never expect to see you anymore

Banks of the Ohio

15

(New Accompaniment)

New Notes:

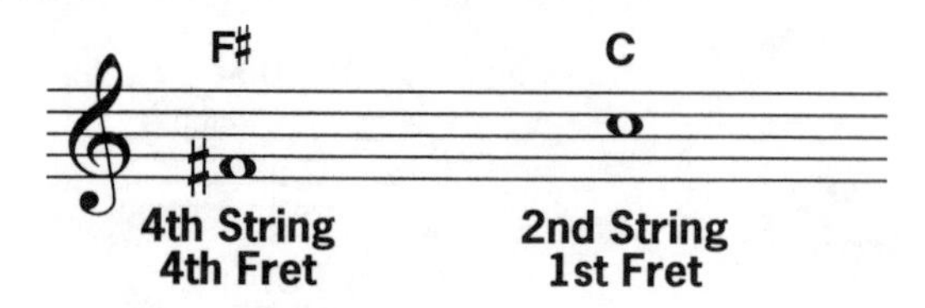

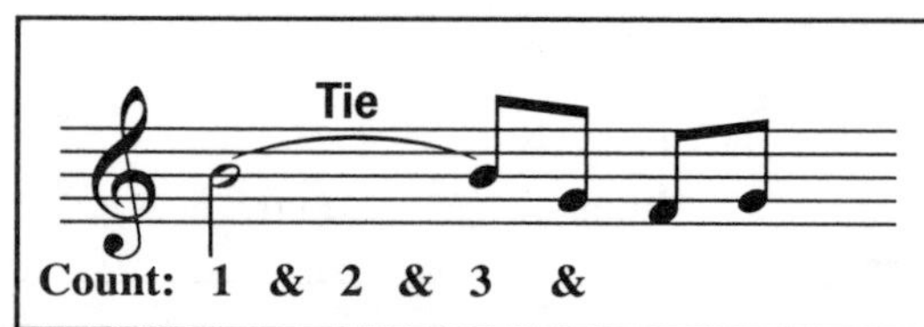

Tie

A tie joins two notes of the same pitch. Play the first note and let it ring throught the time value of the second note.

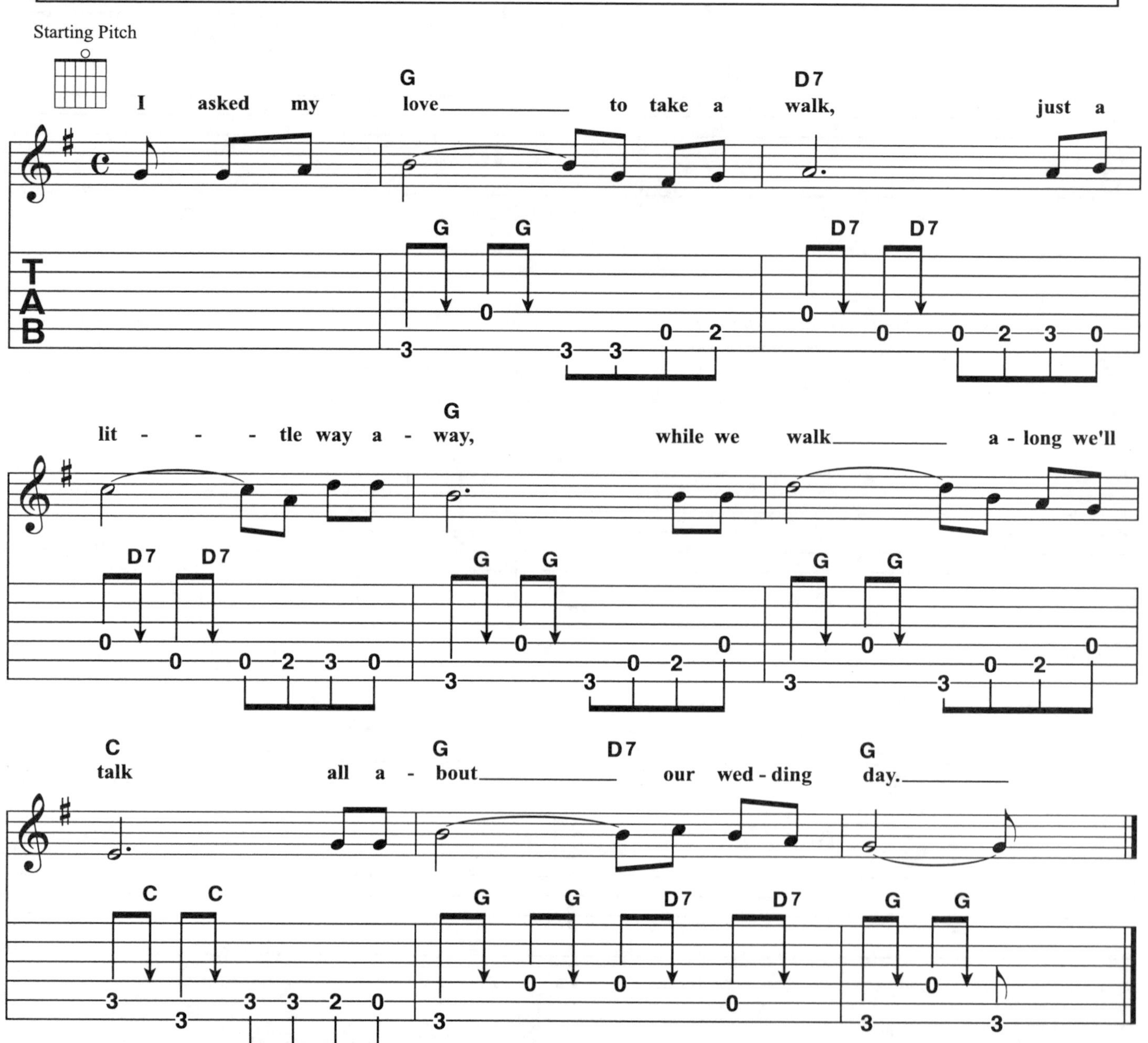

2. **Only say that you'll be mine**
   and in our home we'll happy be,
   down beside where the waters flow,
   on the banks of the Ohio.

Bury Me Beneath the Willow
16
New Note
E
1st String Open
Starting Pitch
My heart is sad and I am lone - ly for the on - ly one I love, when
shall I see her, oh, no nev - er, 'till we meet in heav'n a - bove.
Oh, bu - ry me be - neath the wil - low, un - der the weeping wil - low tree. So
she will know where I am sleep - ing, and per - haps she'll weep for me.

Precious Memories

Starting Pitch
17
G C G D7
Pre-cious mem - 'ries, un - seen an - gels, sent from some-where to my soul.
G C G D7 G
How they lin - ger ev - er near me, and the sa-cred past un - fold.
G C G
Pre - cious mem - 'ries how they lin - ger, how they ev - er flood my soul.
C G D7 G
In the still - ness of the mid - night, pre - cious, sa-cred scenes un - fold.
T
A
B

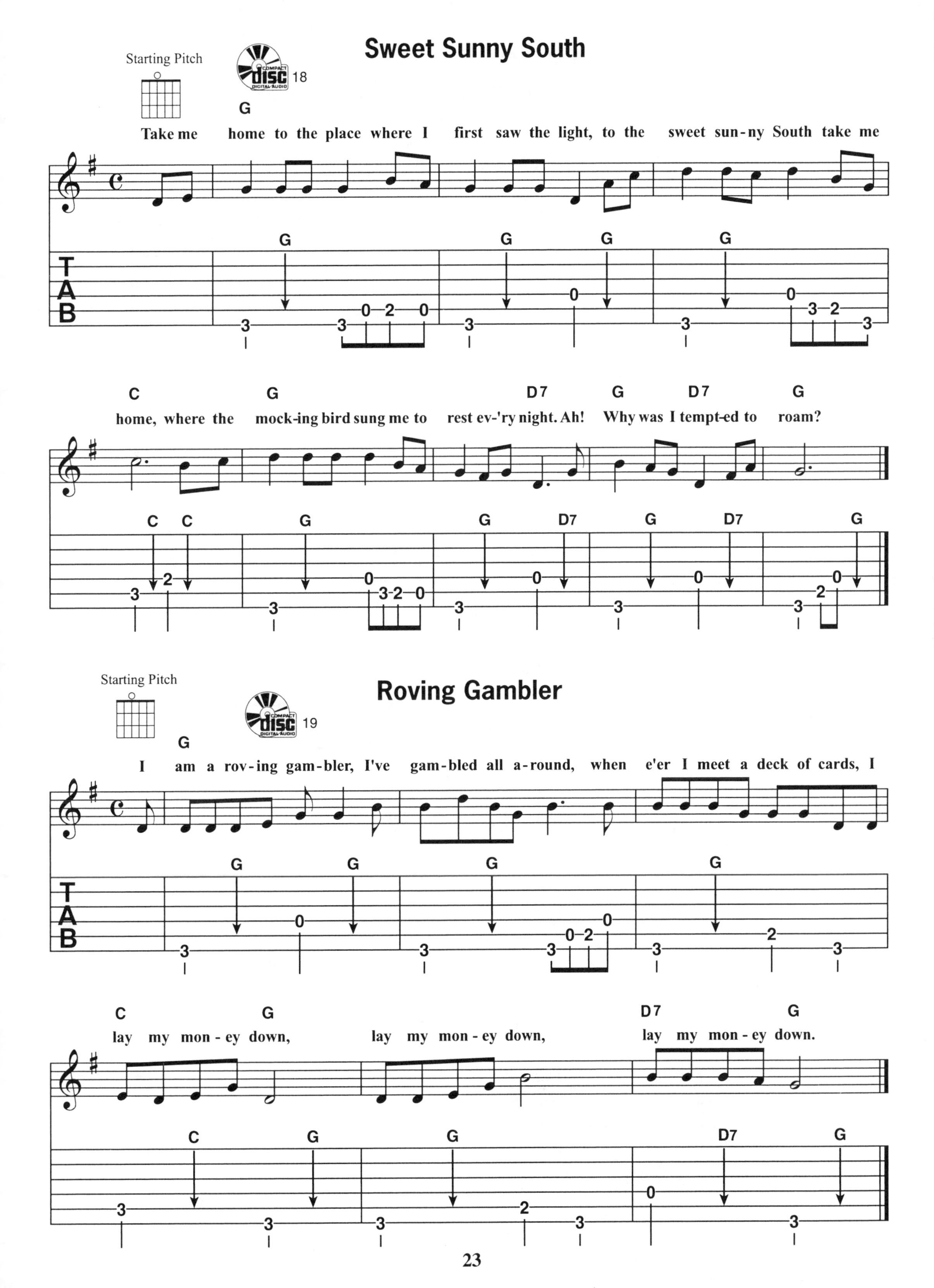
Sweet Sunny South
Starting Pitch
18
Take me home to the place where I first saw the light, to the sweet sun-ny South take me
home, where the mock-ing bird sung me to rest ev-'ry night. Ah! Why was I tempt-ed to roam?
Roving Gambler
Starting Pitch
19
I am a rov-ing gam-bler, I've gam-bled all a-round, when e'er I meet a deck of cards, I
lay my mon-ey down, lay my mon-ey down, lay my mon-ey down.

Bluegrass Solos

Remember: Lines = Strings
Numbers = Frets

Tab Note Value Review

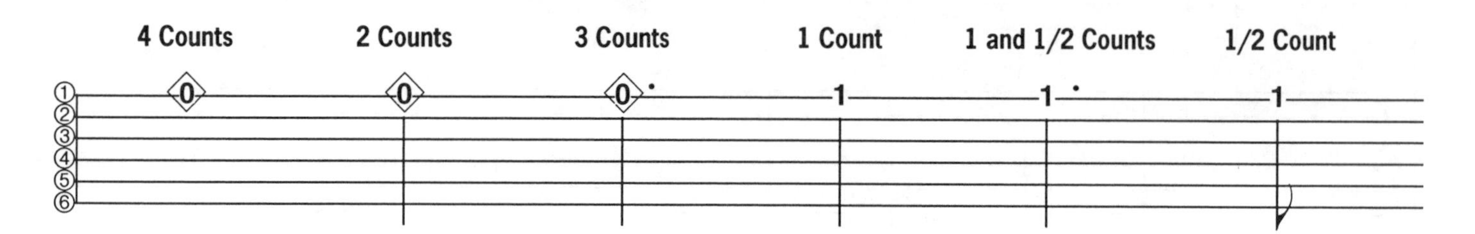

Cotton–Eyed Joe

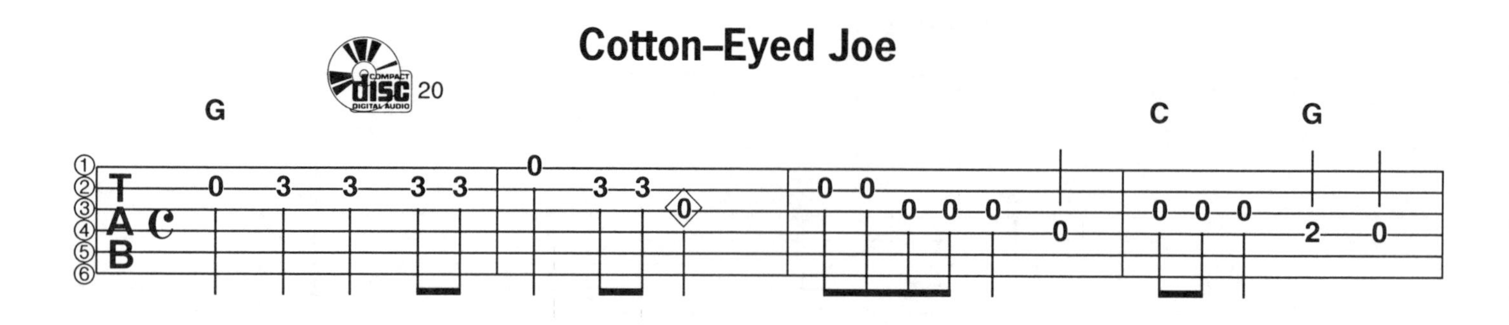

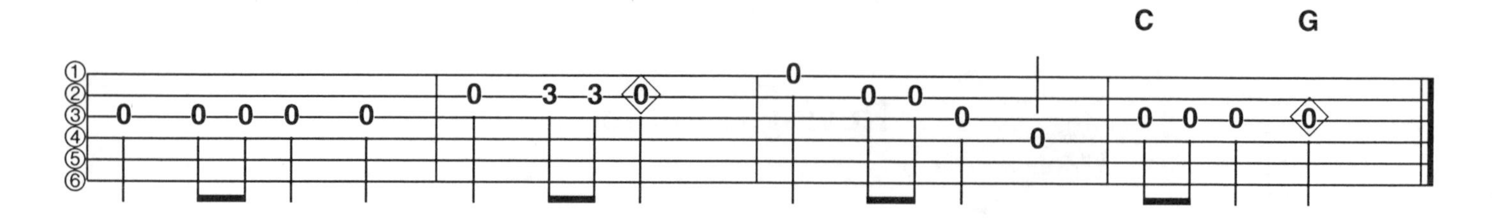

Poor Ellen Smith

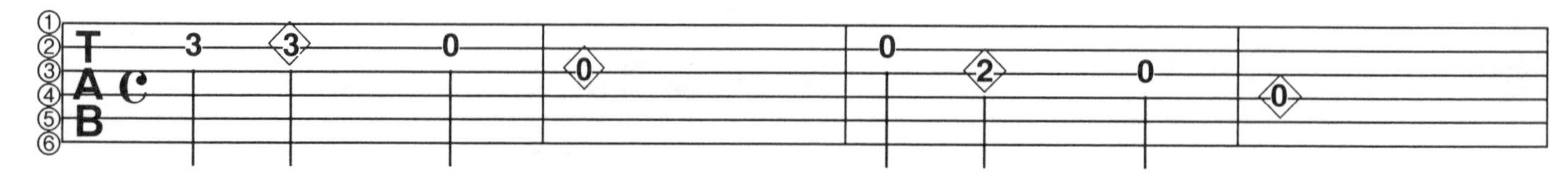

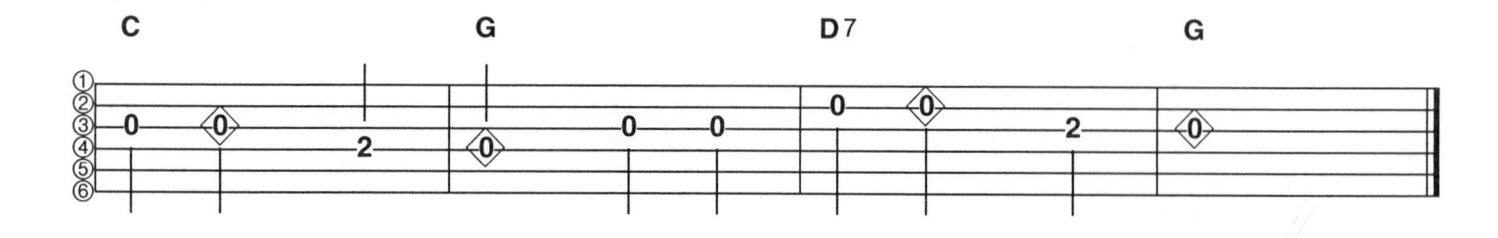

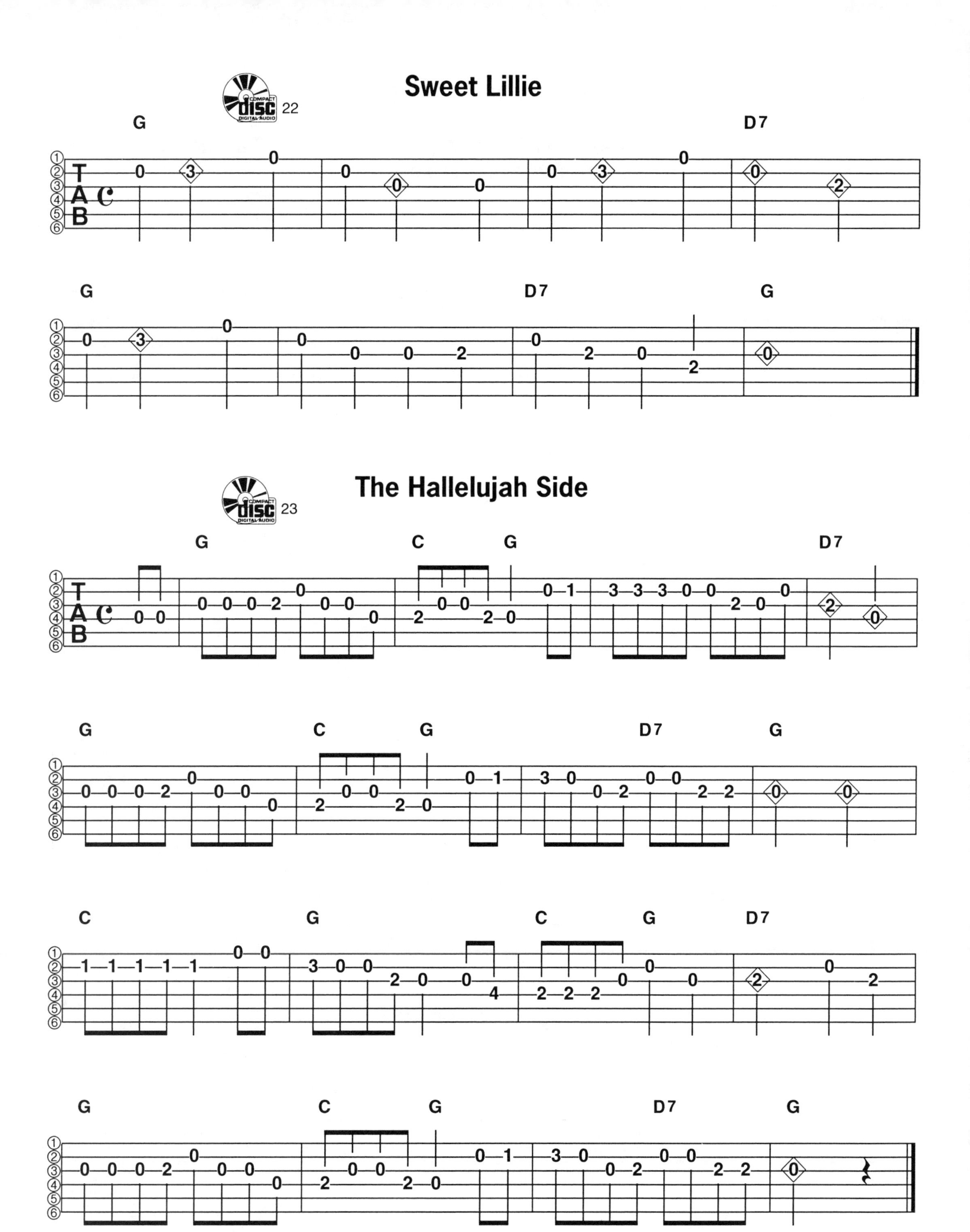
Sweet Lillie
22
G
D7
G
D7
G
The Hallelujah Side
23
G
C
G
D7
G
C
G
D7
G
C
G
C
G
D7
G
C
G
D7
G

Hammer–On

A "Hammer On" is a technique used often in Country music. When we "hammer–on" we pick the first note and while it is still ringing we finger another note.

Examples:

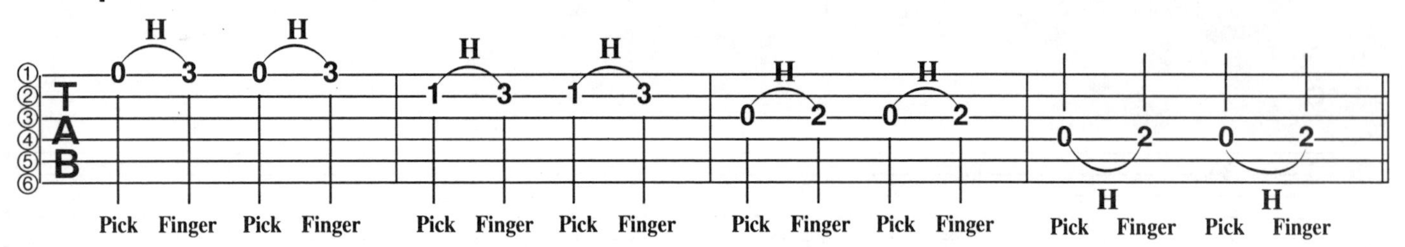

Short Life of Trouble

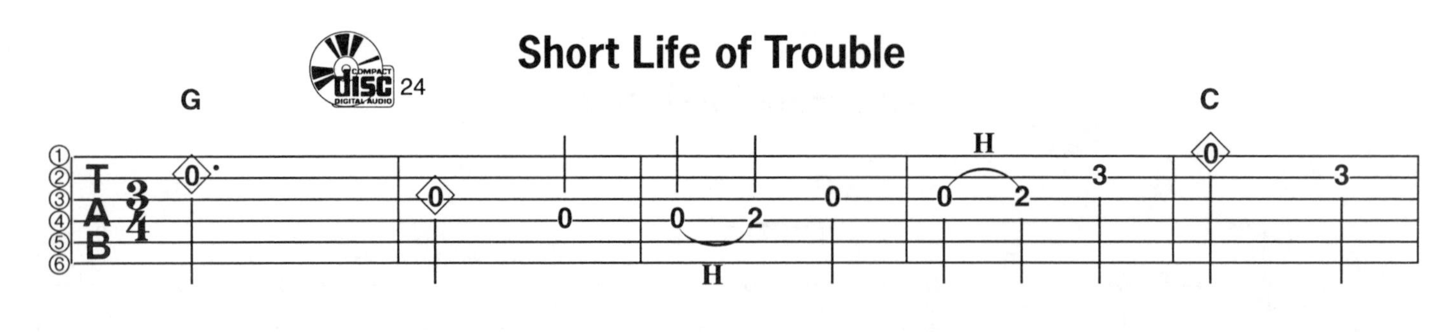

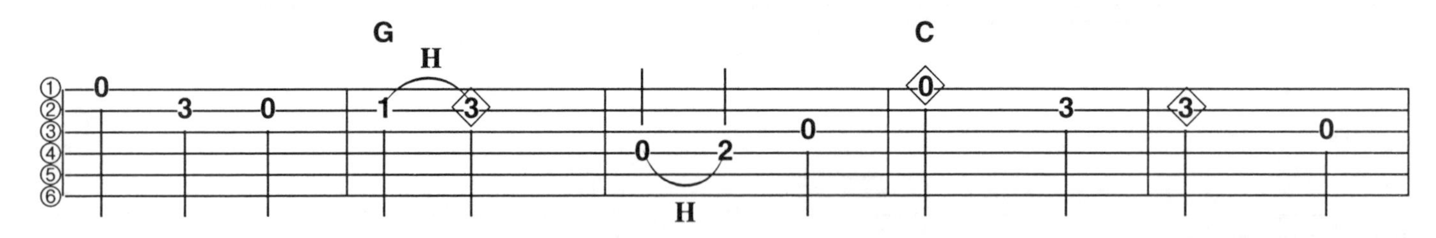

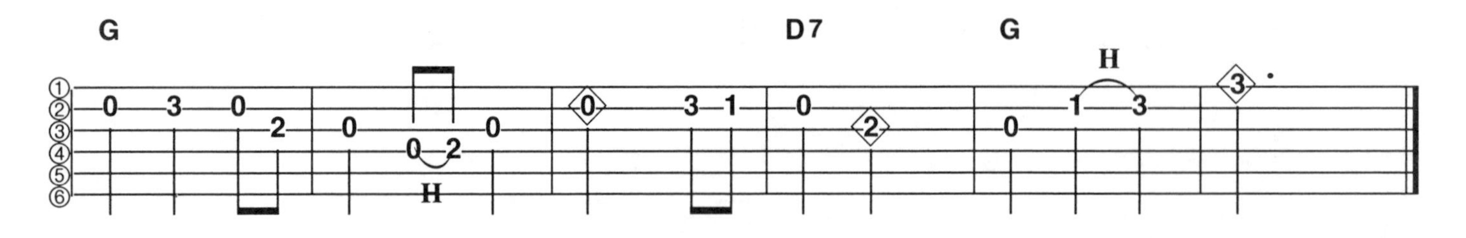

Golden Hammer

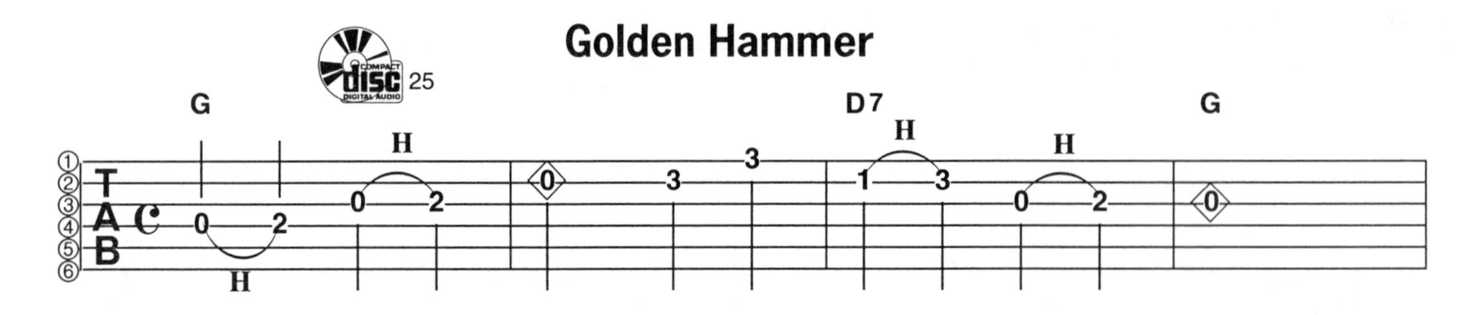

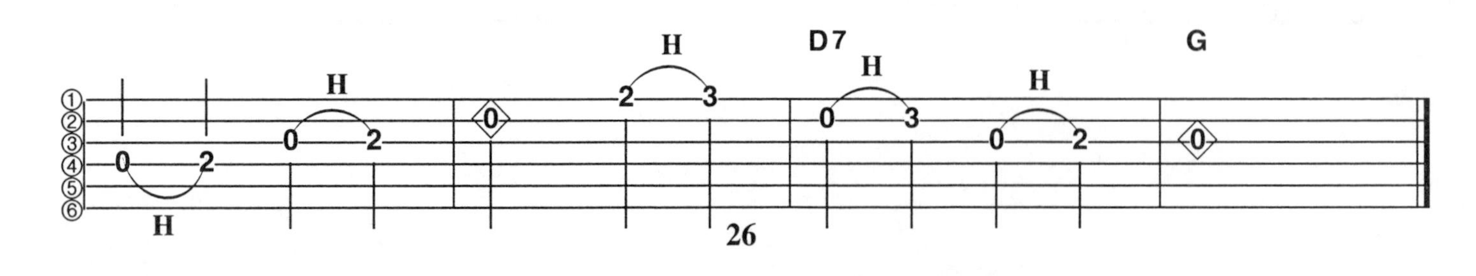

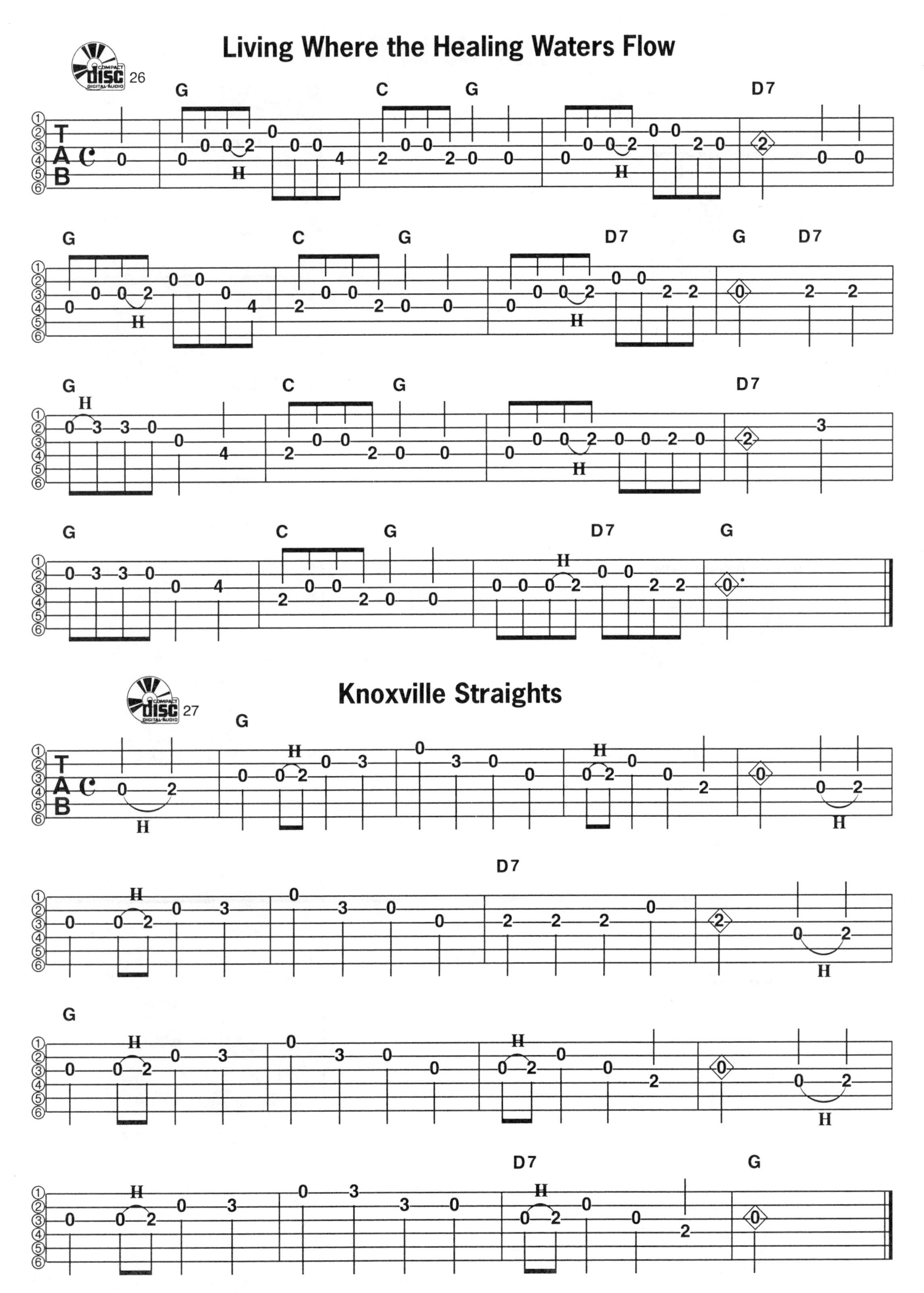
Living Where the Healing Waters Flow
COMPACT disc DIGITAL AUDIO 26
Knoxville Straights
COMPACT disc DIGITAL AUDIO 27

Chords in D

D

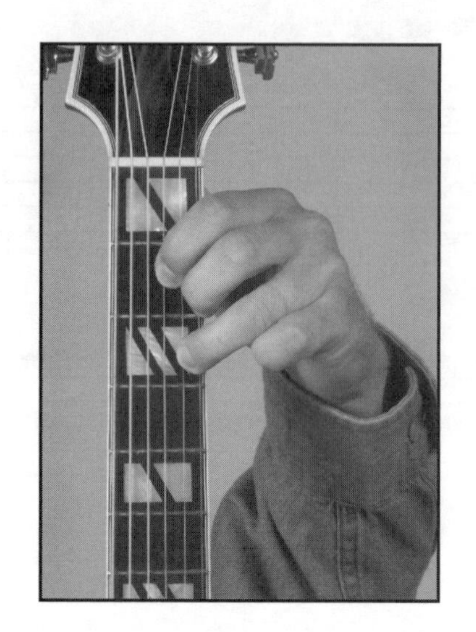

G

A7

Little Bessie

Note to Learn

28

Low A

5th String Open

Starting Pitch

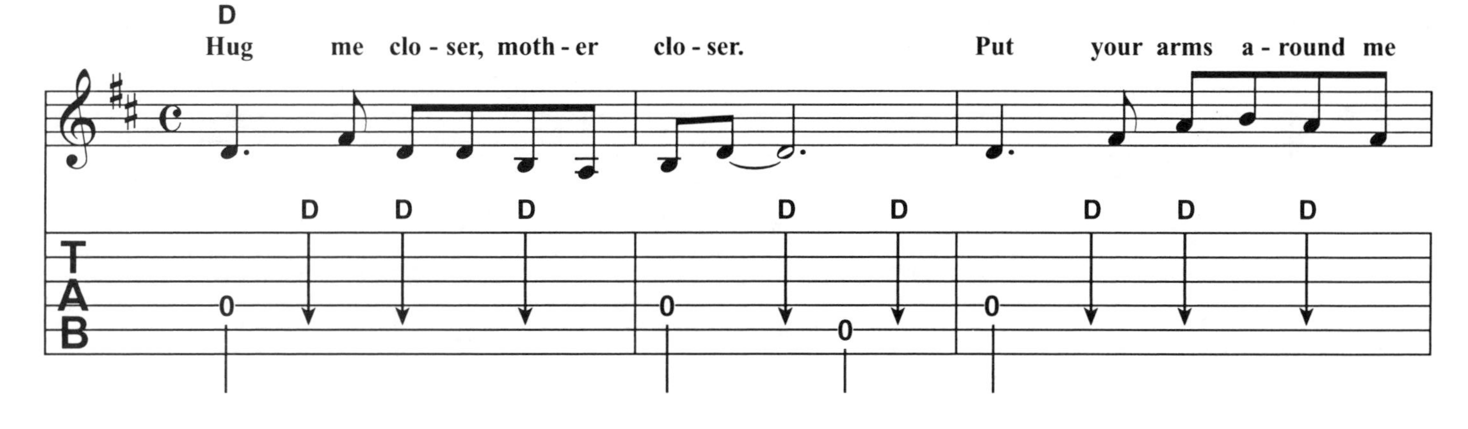

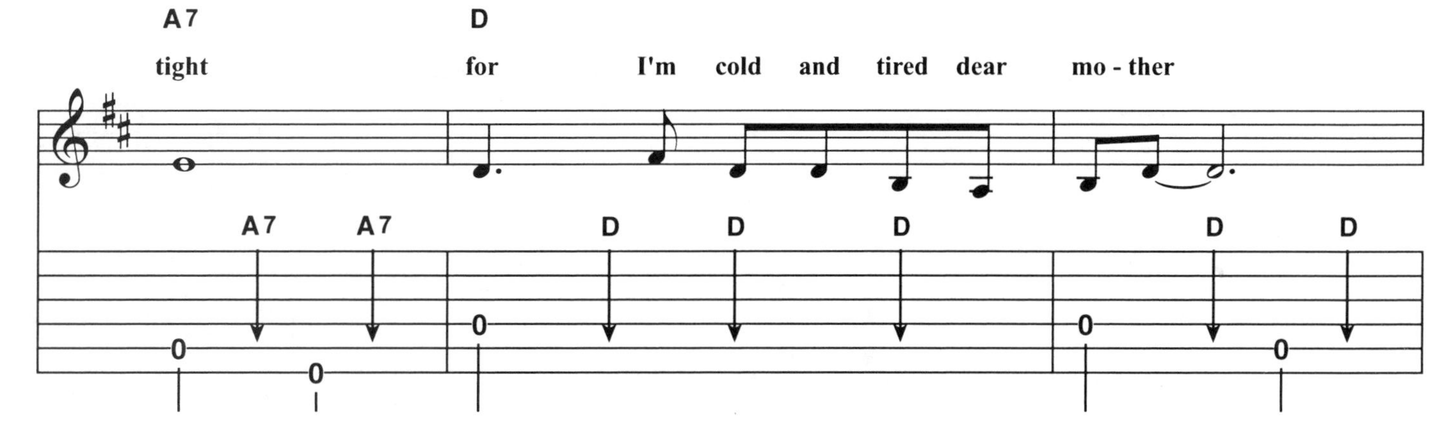

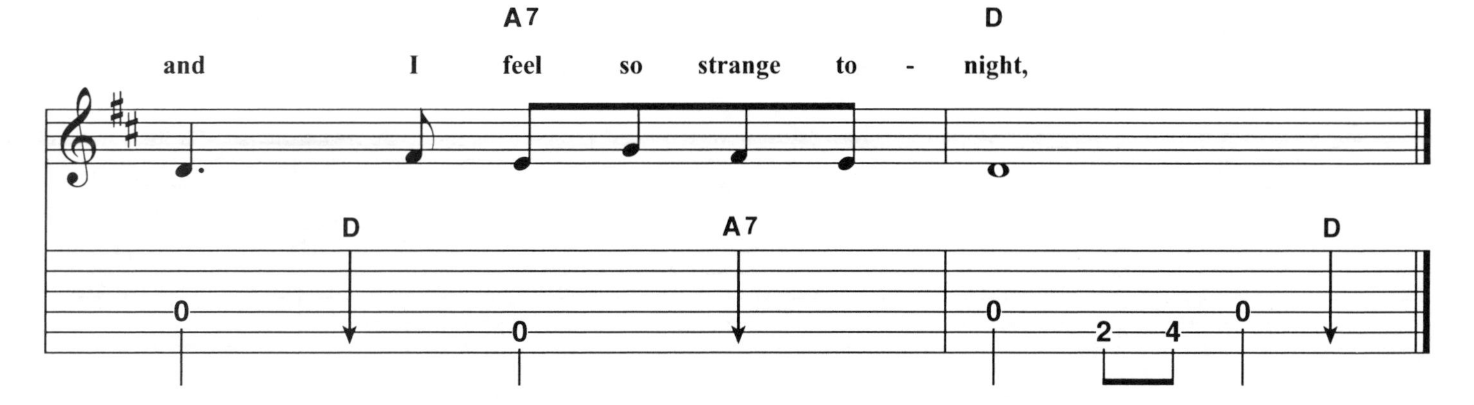

2. Something hurts me here, dear mother
Like a stone upon my breast
And I wonder, mother, wonder
Why it is I cannot rest.

3. Just before the lamps were lighted
Just before the chidren came
While the room was very quiet
I heard someone call my name.

4. Come up here my Little Bessie,
Come up here and live with me
Where little children never suffer,
Through the long eternity.

5. Now up yonder at the portal,
That are shining very fair
Little Bessie now is tended
By the Savior's loving care.

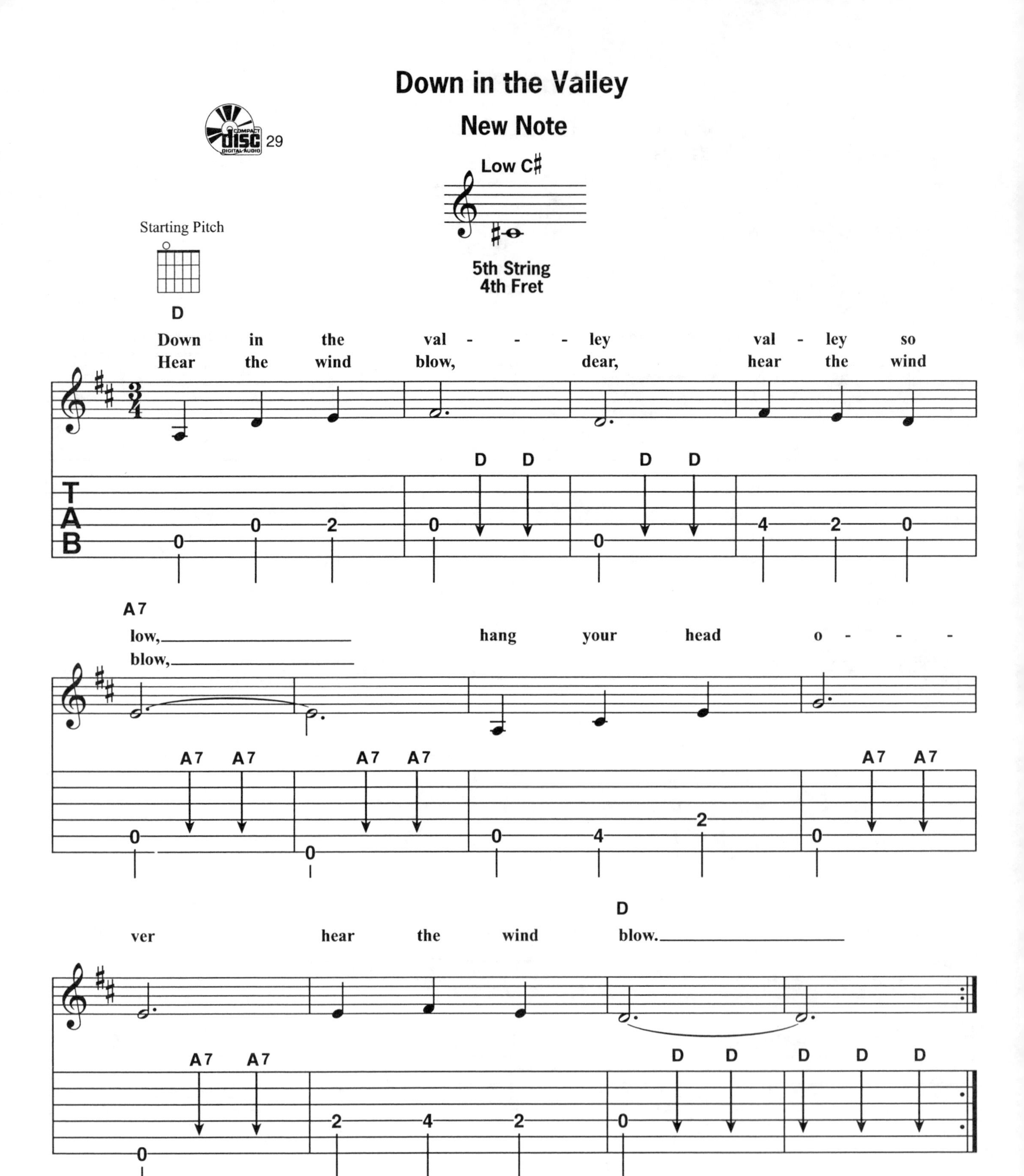

2. Violets love sunshine, roses love dew,
Angels in Heaven know I love you,
Know I love you, dear, know I love you,
Angels in Heaven know I love you.

New River Train

2. Darling you can't love two,
   Darling you can't love two,
   You can't love two and still be true,
   Darling, you can't love two.

3. Darling you can't love many,
   Darling you can't love many,
   You can't love many or you won't have any,
   Darling, you can't love many.

When You and I Were Young, Maggie
Starting Pitch
31
D G D A7
I wan-dered to-day to the hill, Mag-gie, to watch the scene be - low. The
D G G D A7
D G D A7 D
creek and the old rus-ty mill, Mag-gie, where we sat in the long, long a - go. The
D G D A7 D
G D A7
green grove is gone from the hill, Mag-gie, where first the dai-sies had sprung. The
G G G G D D D D A7 A7 A7 A7 A7
D G D A7 D
old rus-ty mill is now still, Mag-gie, since you and I were young.
D G G D D D
H

Uncle Joe

D
Did you ev-er go to meet-in' Un-cle Joe, Un-cle Joe? Did you ev-er go to meet-in' Un-cle

D D D D D

A7 D
Joe? Did you ev-er go to meet-in' Un-cle Joe, Un-cle Joe? I

G D
don't mind the weath-er if the

A7 D D D G D

A7 D
wind don't blow.

Chorus

Hop high la-dies cakes all_ dough. Hop high la-dies

A7
cakes all_ dough.

A7 D D D D D A7 A7

D
Hop high la - dies cakes all_ dough. I

G D
don't mind the weath-er if the

A7 D
wind don't blow.

D D D G D A7 D

In the Pines

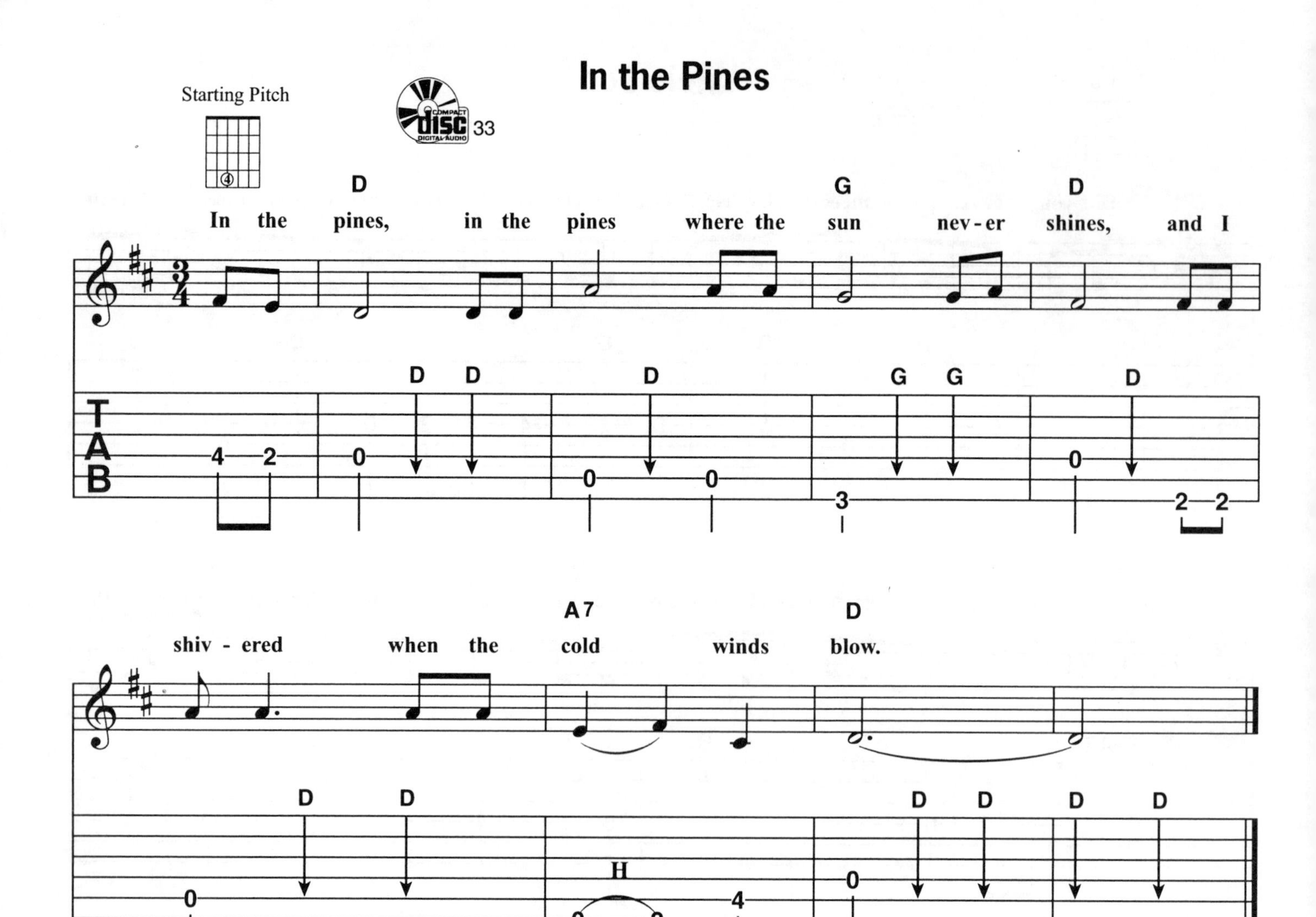

2. The longest train I ever saw,
   Went down that Georgia line.
   The engine passed at six o'clock
   And the cab went by at nine.

3. I asked my captain for the time of day,
   He said he throwed his watch away.
   It's a long steel rail and a short cross ties,
   I'm on my way back home.

Solos in D

Cripple Creek

Mountain Spring

W. Bay

Pull Off

The "Pull Off" is the opposite of the "Hammer On". With a Pull Off, we finger a note, pick it, and while it sounds, pull our finger off to an open string or to a note of a lower pitch.

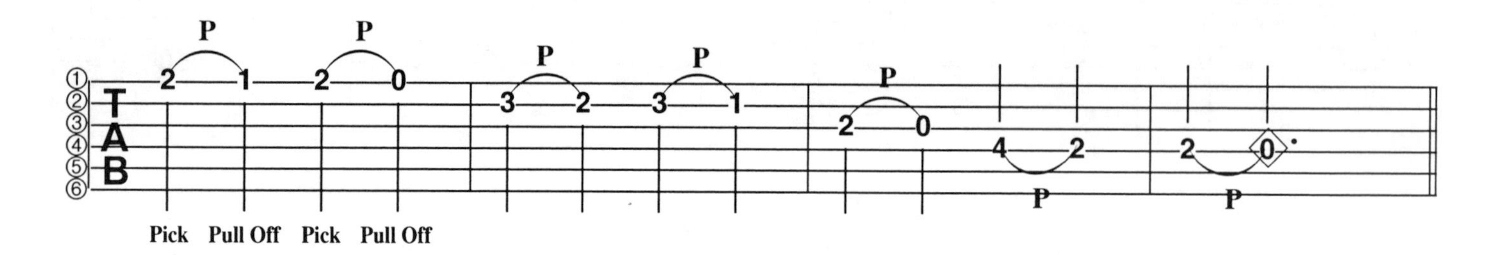

Nine Pound Hammer

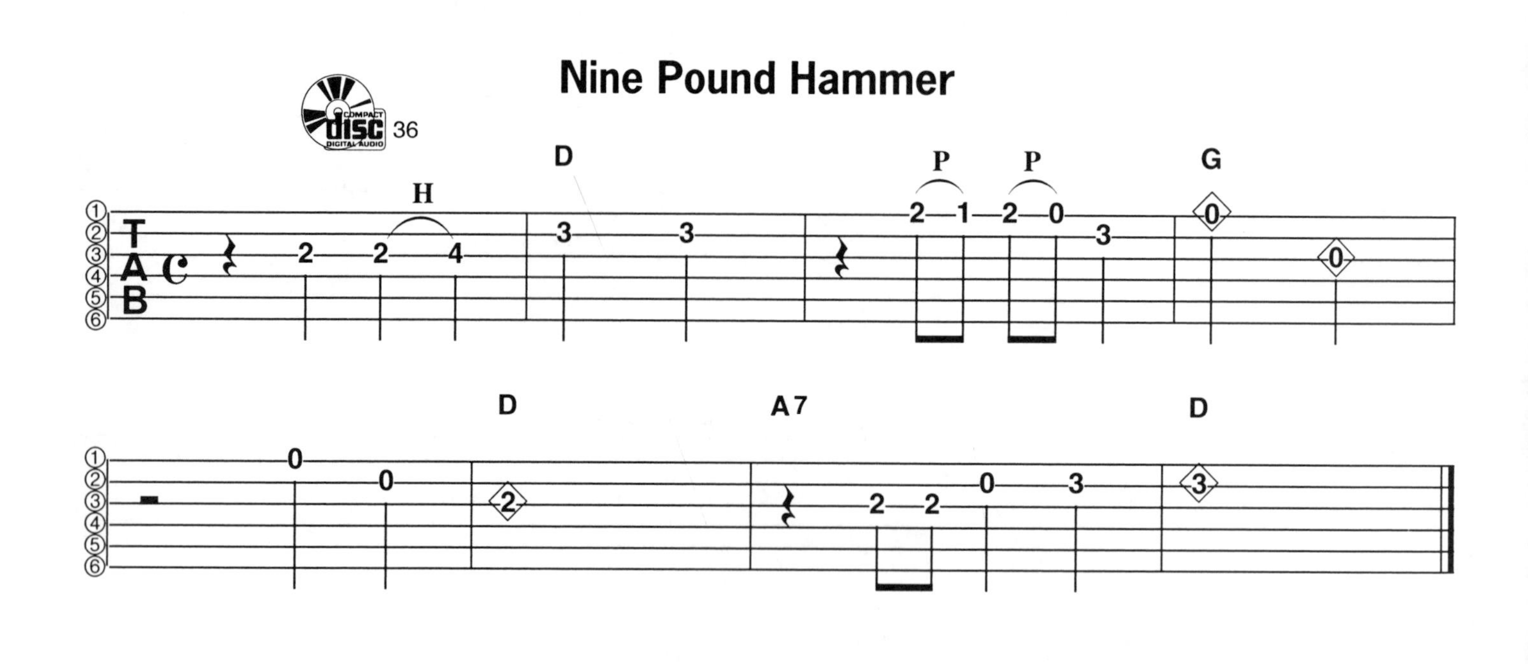

Reuben's Train

Using Hammer–On and Pull–Off

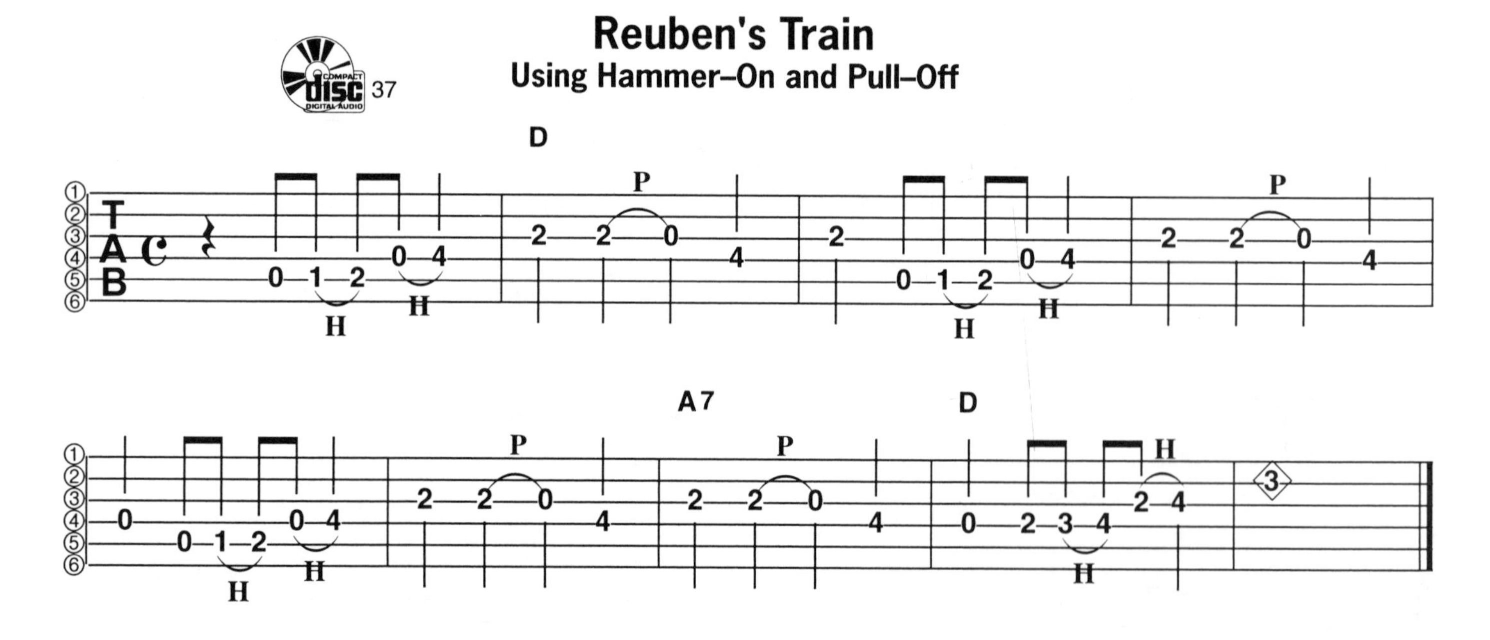

Cluck Old Hen

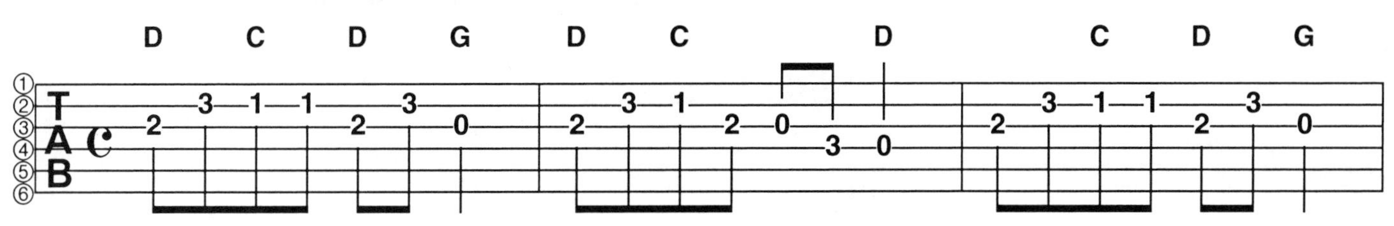

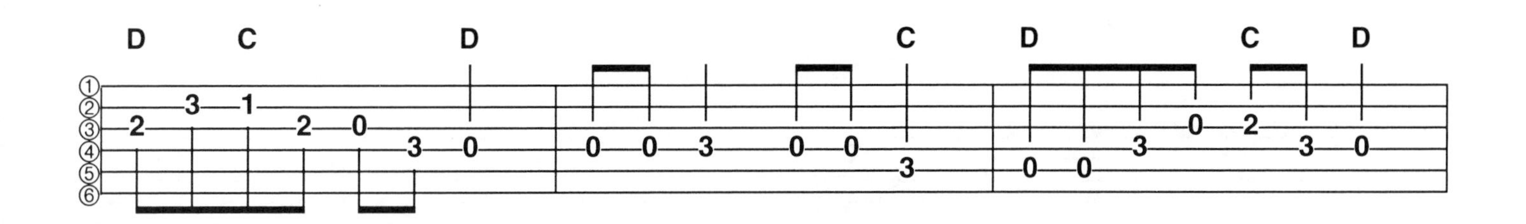

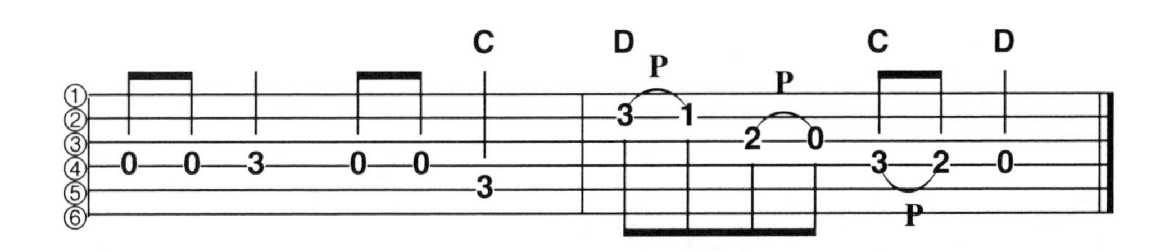

White House Blues

39

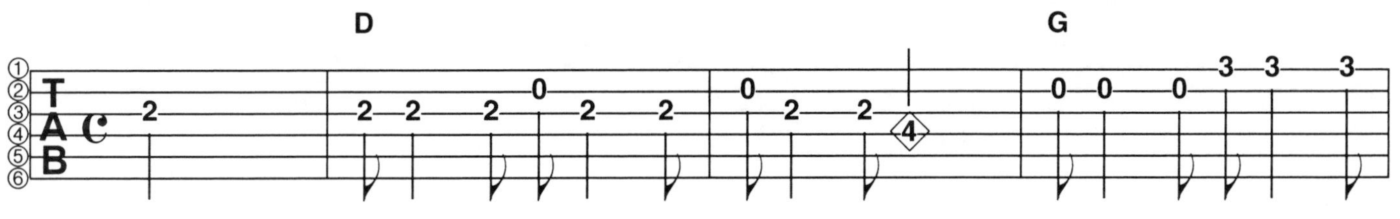

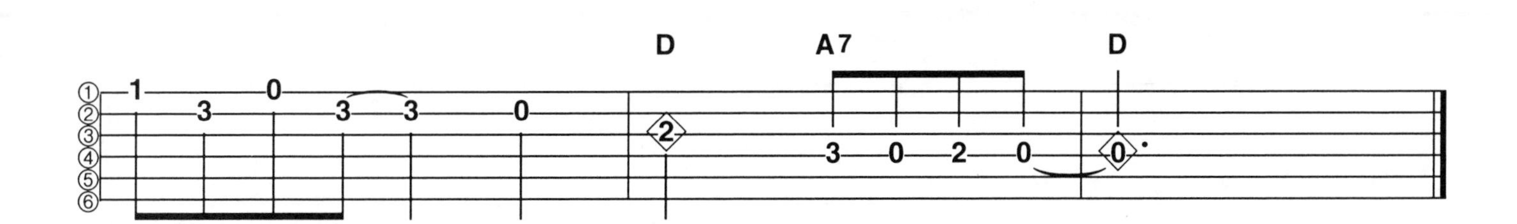

The Slide

With a Slide you play a note and then slide your finger up or down to a different note on the *same* string.

Slide Study #1

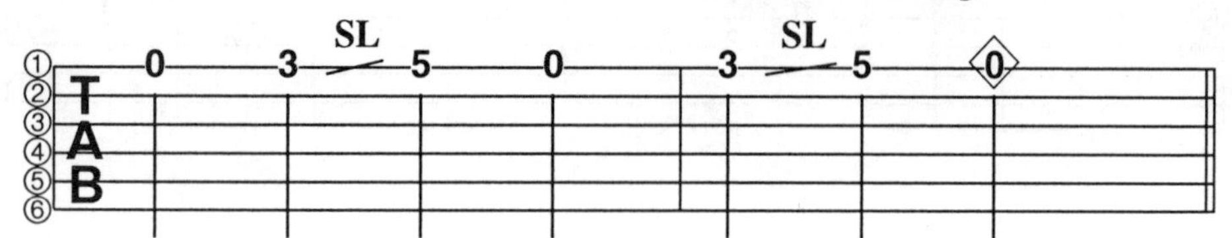

Slide Study #2

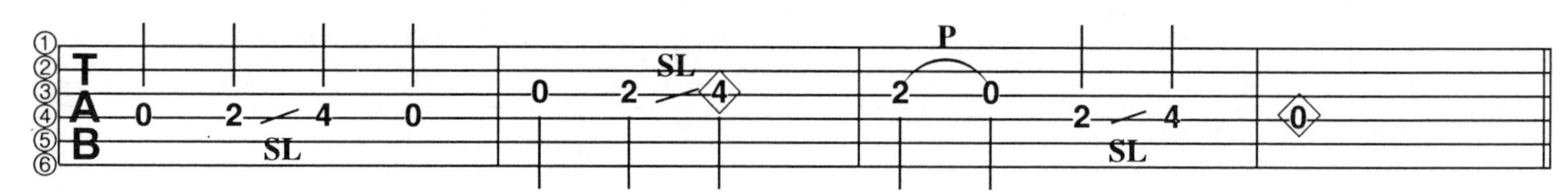

My Old Cottage Home

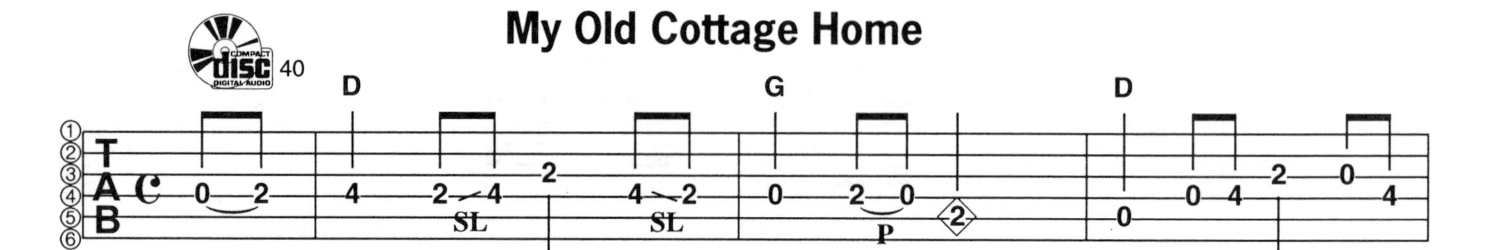

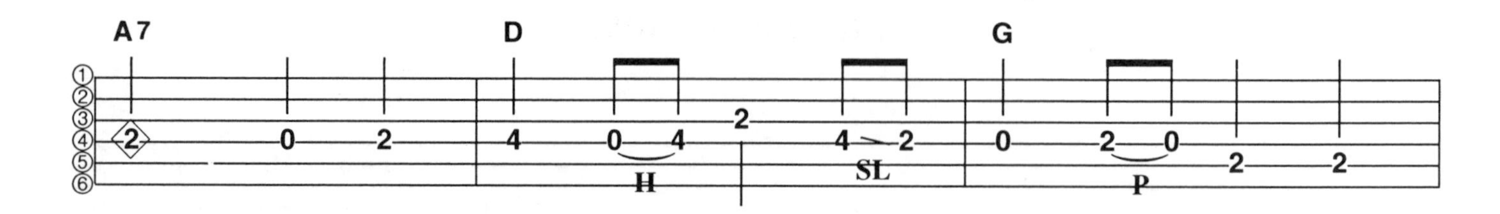

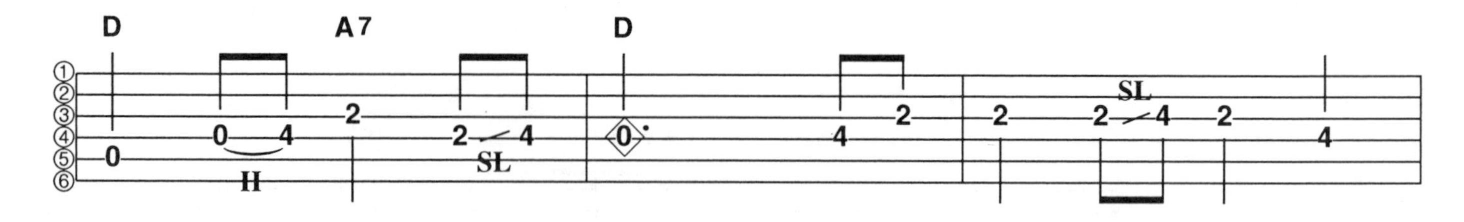

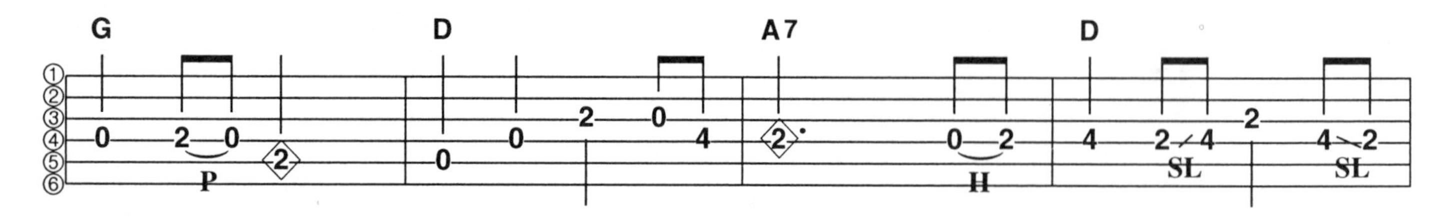

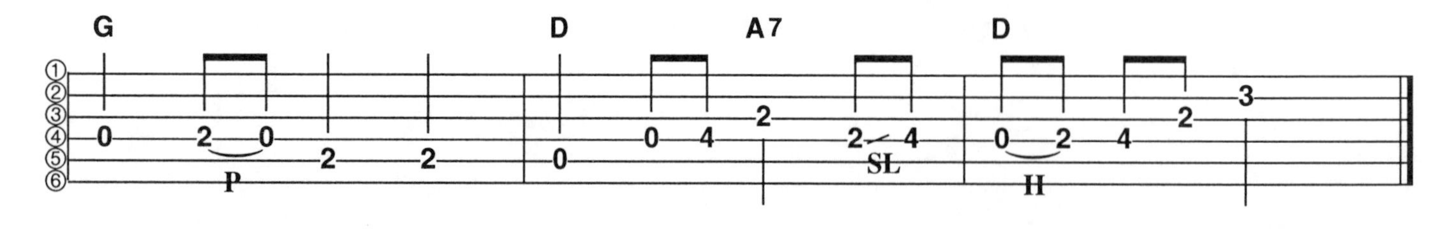

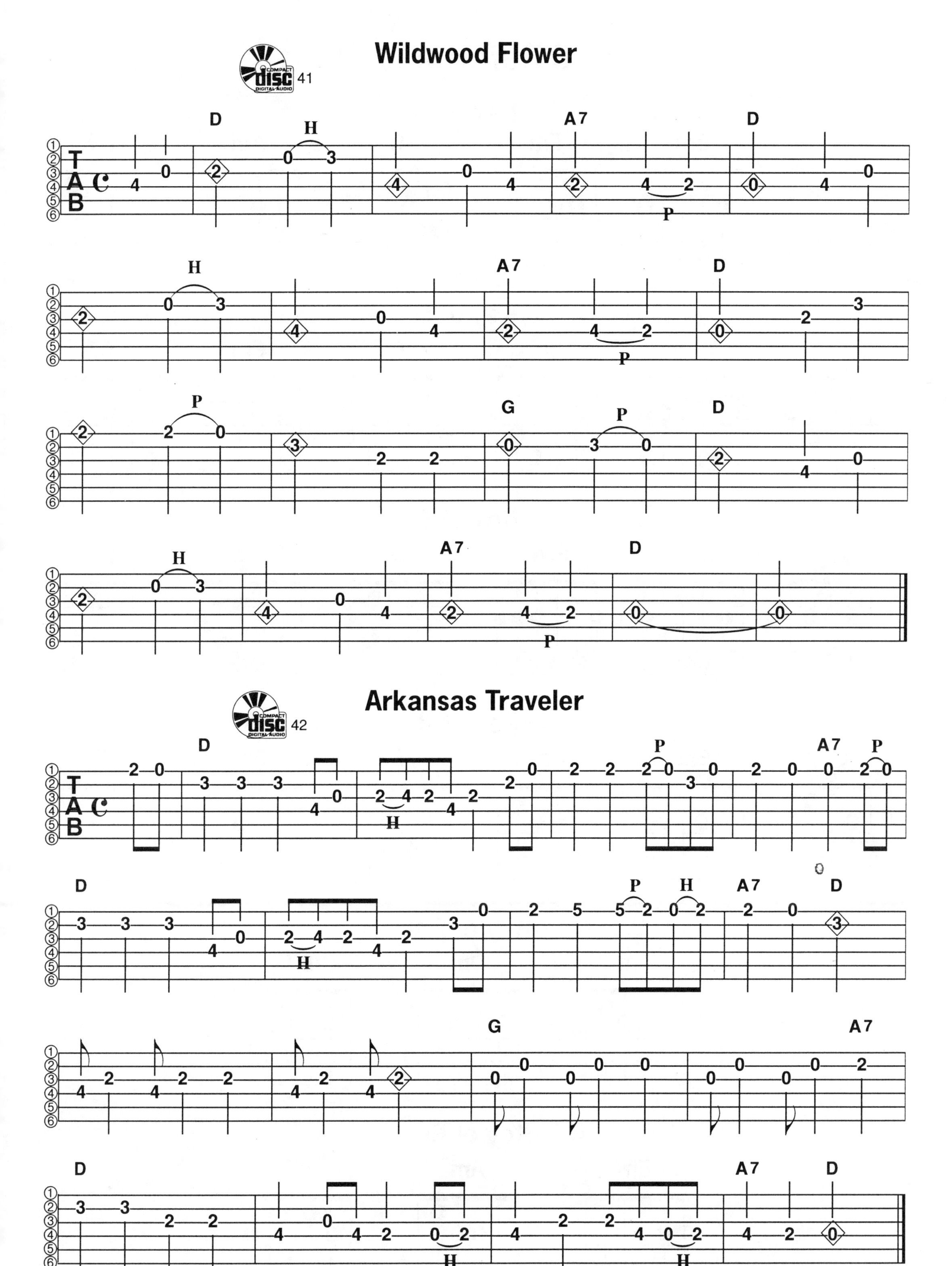
Wildwood Flower
41
Arkansas Traveler
42

Chord Reference Chart

Key of G

G
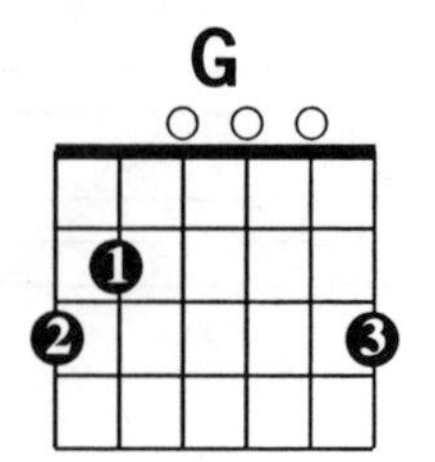

Bm
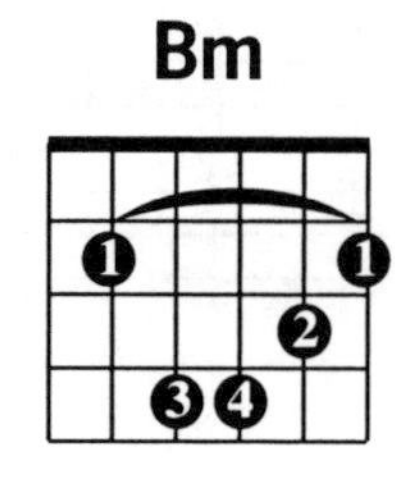

Em
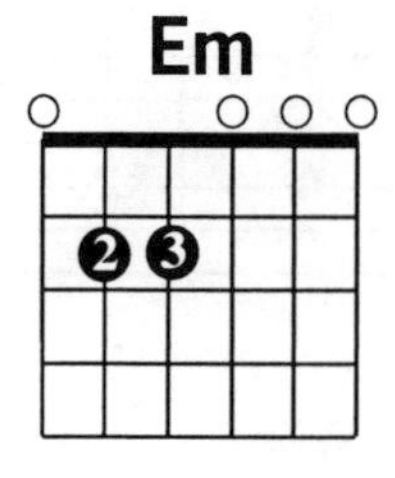

C
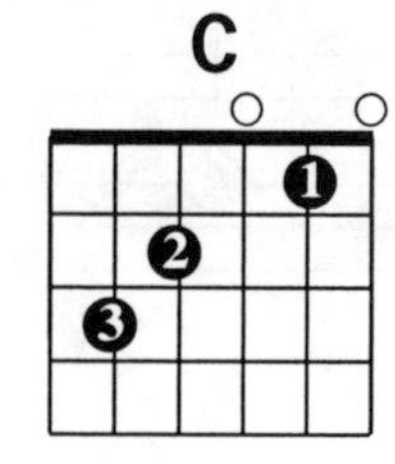

Am
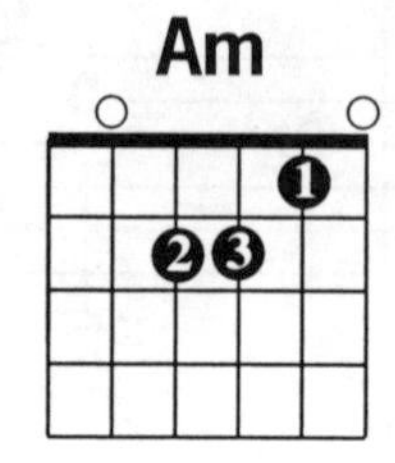

D7
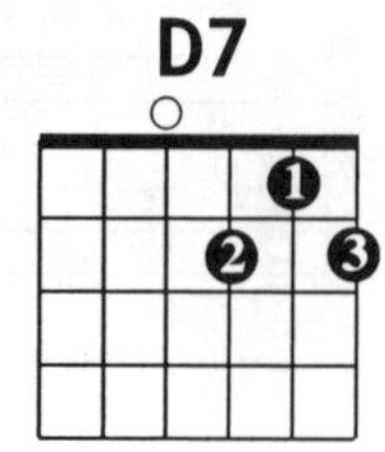

Key of D

D
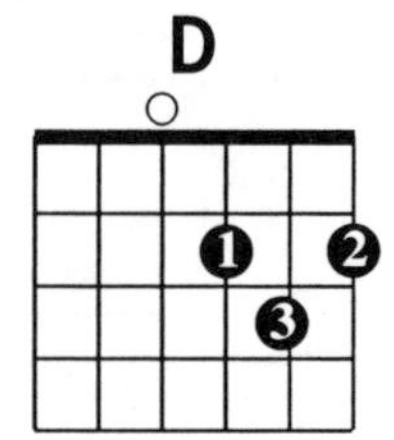

F♯m
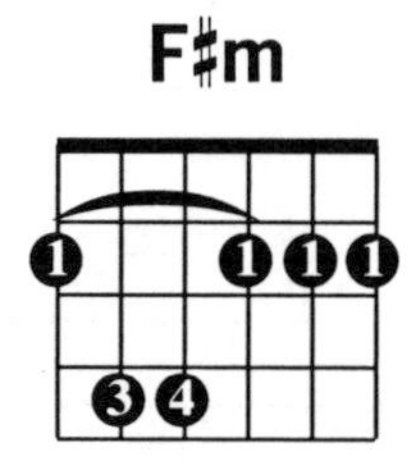

Bm
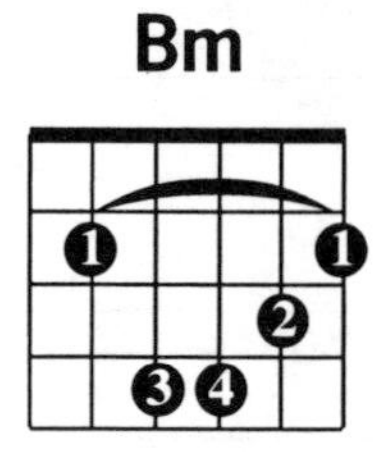

G
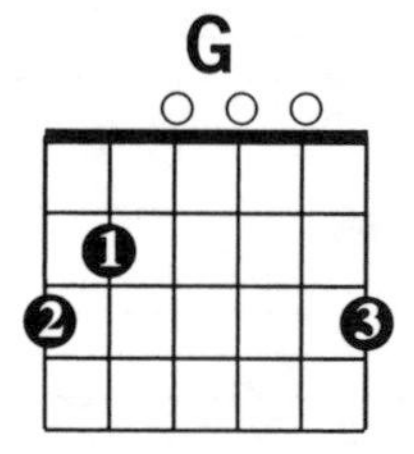

Em
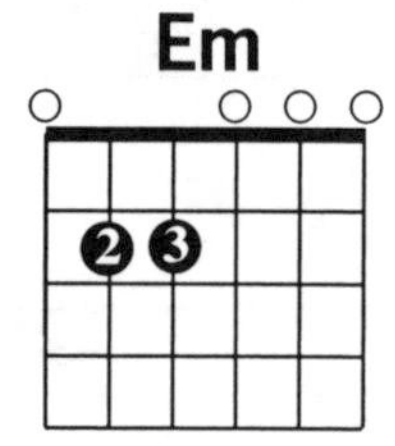

A7
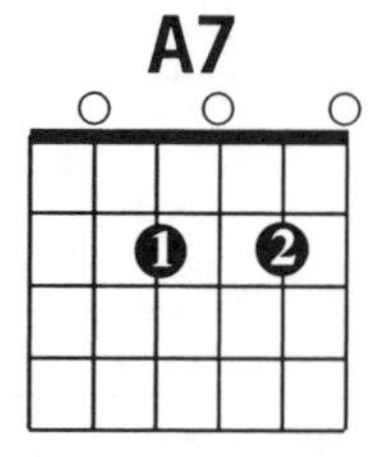

Key of A

A
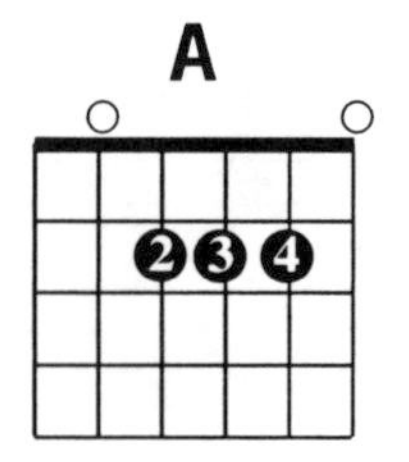

C♯m
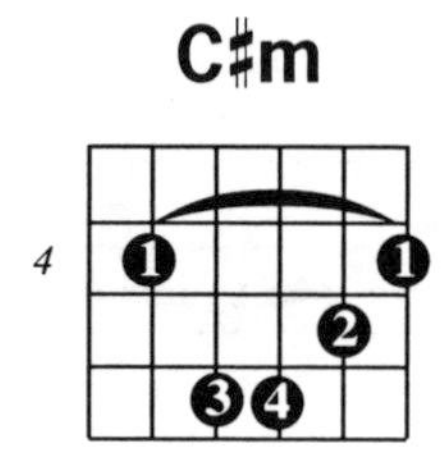

F♯m
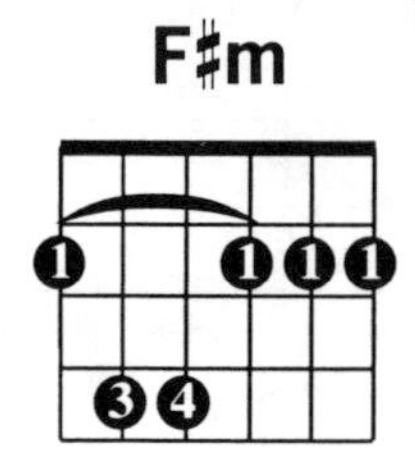

D
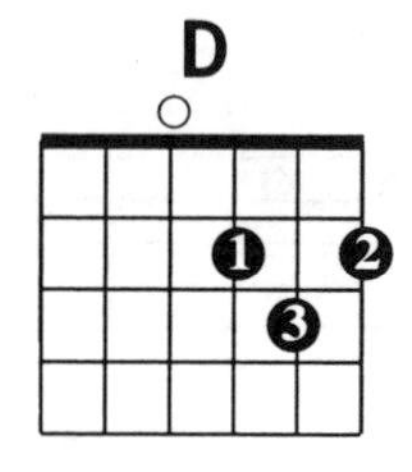

Bm
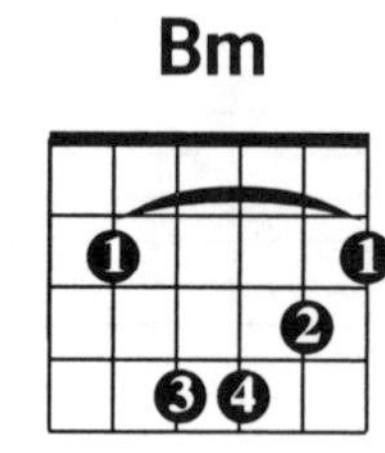

E7
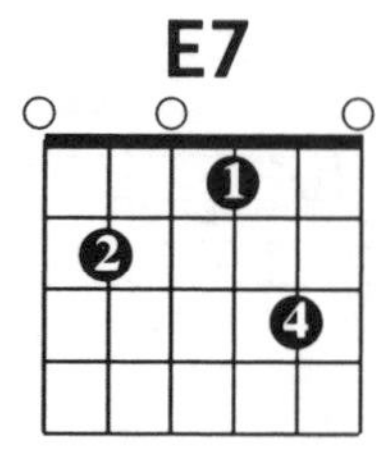

Key of C

C
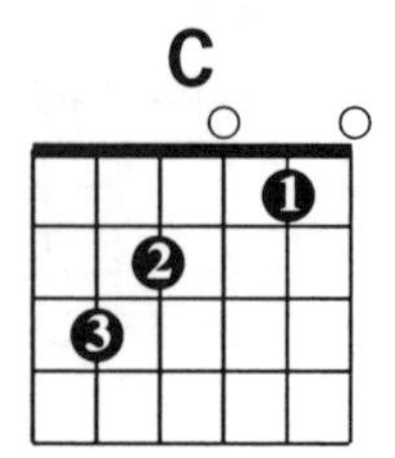

Em
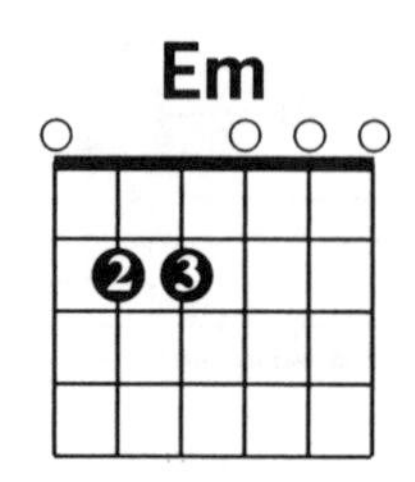

Am
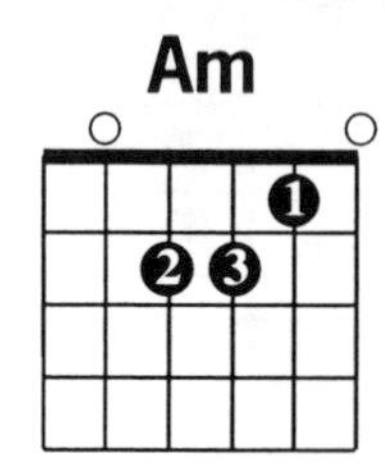

F
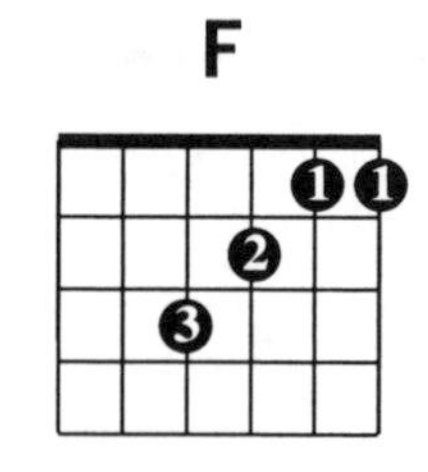

Dm
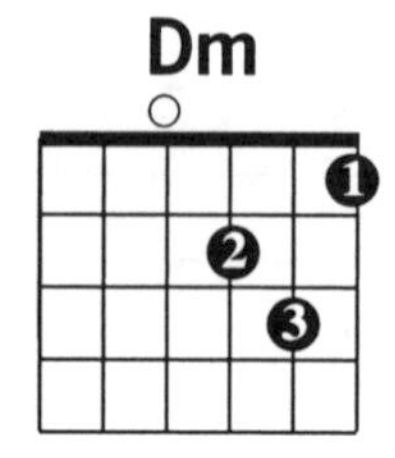

G7
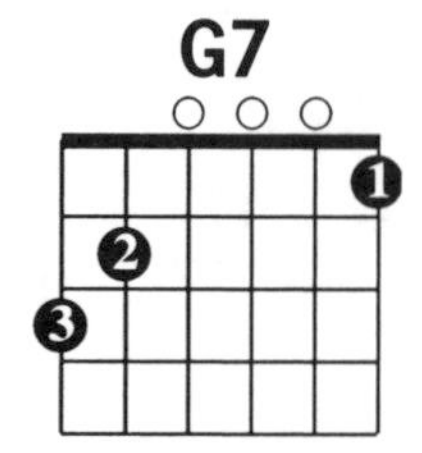

Key of Am

Am
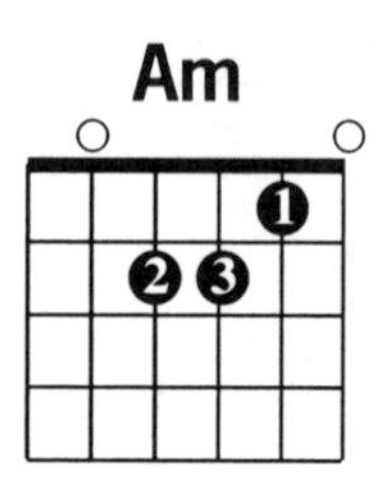

Dm
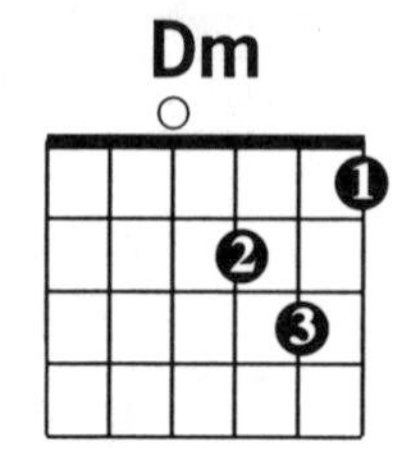

E7
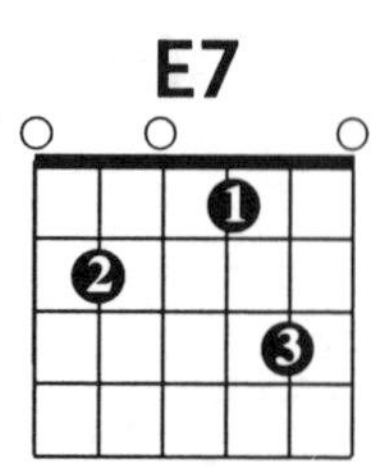

Key of Em

Em
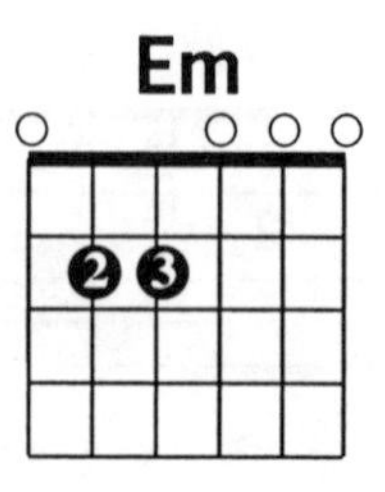

Am
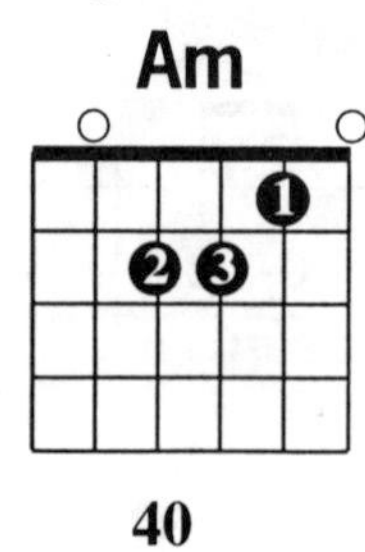

B7
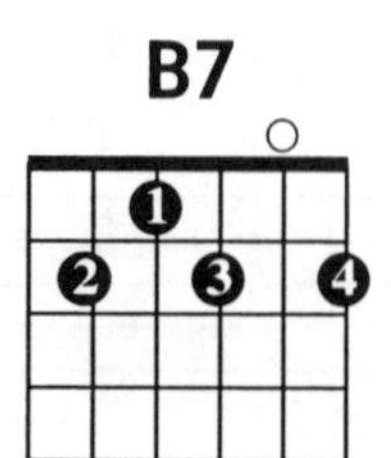